HISTORY'S MOST

DANGEROUS JOBS

NAVVIES

HISTORY'S MOST DANGEROUS JOBS

DANGEROUS JOBS

NAVVIES

ANTHONY BURTON

Images facing title page. Top: Men working on lock restoration in the twentieth century. Little has changed since the canal was built. (British Waterways); *bottom*: Men being lowered down a shaft in Kilsby Tunnel, on the London & Birmingham Railway. (National Railway Museum, York)

First published 2012

The History Press
The Mill, Brimscombe Port
Stroud, Gloucestershire, GL5 2QG
www.thehistorypress.co.uk

British Library Cataloguing in Publication Data.
A catalogue record for this book is available from the British Library.

ISBN 978 0 7524 7961 3

Typesetting and origination by The History Press
Printed in Great Britain

CONTENTS

Navvies at work on the Great Central Railway. (Leicestershire Record Office)

INTRODUCTION

This is a subject that has a very special place in my life. When I first started writing books some forty years ago I had seen myself as a humourist. The first book was a success, but the second sank without a trace, so my agent Murray Pollinger suggested that I might think of trying something different. He asked a very good question: 'What book have you read recently that you wish you had written yourself?' I had an instant answer – Terry Coleman's *The Railway Navvies*. Murray asked if there was anything similar that I might want to write myself and I said that no one had ever really researched the story of the earlier navvies, who had built the canals. There was not enough material for a book just on canal navvies so I broadened the scope to include everyone involved in canal construction, from engineers to administrators. The result was *The Canal Builders*, which is still in print and in its fourth edition. Later I was invited to write a similar book on railway construction, *The Railway Builders*, and that involved me doing more research that included the railway navvies. Finally I was invited to write about the railways the British had built overseas, *The Railway Empire*, and that led me to look at the work of British navvies who went to work abroad, everywhere from Europe to Australia. This book is an attempt to bring these three themes together as a single narrative, describing the life and work of a remarkable group of workmen who built vital transport systems around the world.

In writing civil engineering history the author is faced with a dilemma. We have moved to a metric system but in the eighteenth and nineteenth centuries everyone used the old imperial measures – feet and inches, pounds and ounces and so on. It seems absurd to say, for example, that when George Stephenson set the standard gauge for British railways he decided on a figure of 143.5cm as the distance the rails should be apart. He didn't – he chose 4ft 8½in. I have therefore used the older units when referring to historic measurements and, of course, these are the units to be found in contemporary documents. The other problem relates to money. Younger readers may need to be reminded that this was the age of pounds, shillings and pence with twenty shillings to the pound and twelve pennies to the shilling. An amount of, for example, two shillings and sixpence could be expressed either as 2s 6d or 2/6. There is inevitably another problem when dealing with money – a shilling in 1760 was only the equivalent of 5p in modern currency in the sense that it is a twentieth of a pound, but in purchasing power it was worth far more than 5p would be today. By using older currencies I hope it at least reminds readers not to think that the two sums are in any way comparable. At various points in the book I have tried to estimate what the equivalent of, for example, a navvy's pay would be in today's money. There are no absolute equivalents but it might be useful to know that it was estimated in 1810, which is roughly the middle of the period we are going to be looking at, that the basic food budget for a family of six in Lancashire was 14s 1d a week. The food was described as being 'of the simplest kind' and included 17lb of oatmeal, 20lb of bacon and only 2lb of meat and 2lb of bacon.[1] Readers can no doubt work out for themselves what it would cost to provide modest meals for a family of six at today's prices.

When *The Canal Builders* was published in 1972 it carried a dedication to our three children. Now forty years later it seems only appropriate to move the dedication on a generation. This one is for the grandchildren, who are:

Emily, Daniel, James, Ben, Leo, Bibi

CHAPTER ONE

WHO WERE THE NAVVIES?

One clue to the question posed in the chapter title can be found in the name 'navvy' itself. It is short for 'navigator', someone who dug river and canal navigations. But that alone doesn't explain why a separate name was needed for a group of men who were, apparently, simply manual labourers. This nineteenth-century broadsheet ballad *Navvy on the Line* gives one of the key characteristics of navvy life:

> I am a navvy bold, that's tramped the country round, sir,
> To get a job of work, where any can be found, sir.
> I left my native home, my friends and my relations,
> To ramble up and down and work in various stations.[1]

The navvy was not a man who simply lived in a house or cottage and went out to work every day; he was constantly on the move, with no settled home. Another popular song of the day was simply called *The Navigators*.[2] This one gives a picture of the work he did from Monday to Saturday – and what happened at the end of the week. Here are two of the verses:

> On Saturday night we receive our pay;
> It's then to the ale-house we go straightway.
> And each sits his sweetheart upon his knee,
> And we treat them well with the barley brew.

> But when several months are gone and past,
> Those pretty young girls got thick in the waist.
> They run to buy candles, they learn lullabies,
> And wish that they still had their dear banker boys.

This suggests something else that sets the navvy apart – these were men who worked hard and lived hard, without too much concern for conventional morality. Because they were always on the move, they lived outside the rest of society, and people who do that are always liable to be treated with suspicion by those living more settled lives. There was no shortage of critics ready to condemn them and their whole way of life and set them alongside other popular bogeymen:

> In the making of canals, it is the general custom to employ gangs of hands who travel from one work to another and do nothing else.
>
> These banditti known in many parts of England by the name of 'Navies' or 'Navigators', and in others by that of 'Bankers', are generally the terror of the surrounding country; they are as completely a class by themselves as the Gipsies. Possessed of all the daring recklessness of the Smuggler, without any of his redeeming qualities, their ferocious behaviour can only be equalled by the brutality of their language. It may be truly said, their hand is against every man, and before they have been long located, every man's hand is against them; and woe befall any woman, with the slightest share of modesty, whose ears they can assail.
>
> From long being known to each other, they in general act in concert, and put in defiance any local constabulary force; consequently crimes of the most atrocious character are common, and robbery, without an attempt at concealment, has been an everyday occurrence, wherever they have been congregated in large numbers.[3]

From this account, it would appear that the coming of navvies to an area would be about as welcome as the arrival of Genghis Khan and his horde. The truth inevitably lies somewhere in between the balladeer's portrait of a rather happy-go-lucky chap, working hard and having fun, and the dangerous criminal. The question that has not been answered is: why should the navvy be so very different from every other type of labourer working in Britain at that time? What is it about building a canal that makes it unlike constructing a road, or indeed digging the fields on the farms? Was there something about canal work that made those who took it on rougher and tougher than anyone else?

The farm question is easiest to answer. No one could deny that farm work was hard and that the work started when you were young and continued to the day you were no longer able to cope through old age and infirmity. William Cobbett championed the rural way of life and declared his own childhood to have been all but idyllic, but when he came to describe what he actually did as a young boy he told a story of hardship that few today could even imagine:

> I do not remember a time when I did not earn my living. My first occupation was driving the small birds from the turnip seed and the rooks from the peas. When I trudged afield, with my wooden bottle and my satchel over my

shoulder, I was hardly able to climb the gates and stiles, and, at the close of day, to reach home was a task of infinite labour. My next employment was weeding wheat, and leading a single horse at harrowing barley. Hoeing peas followed, and hence I arrived at the honour of joining the reapers in harvest, driving the team and holding the plough. We were all of us strong and laborious, and my father used to boast, that he had four boys, the eldest of whom was but fifteen years old, who did as much work as any three men in the parish of Farnham. Honest pride and happy days![4]

Richard Hillyer, who worked on a farm as a boy in the nineteenth century, paints a far gloomier picture:

Every night I dropped asleep over my supper, and then woke up just enough to crawl upstairs and fall into bed … A black depression spread over me. 'This is what it is going to be from now on,' I thought. 'Lifting, hauling, shoving, trudging about from day to day, nothing else through all the years.'[5]

The Victorians were fond of chocolate box pictures of country life, full of pretty milkmaids and jolly ploughboys. The reality was much closer to Hillyer's portrait. But there were other aspects to farm life that set it apart from that of the navvy. The labourer generally lived in a tied cottage – and as long as the cottage was tied to the farm, so was he and his family, and they became part of a settled community that shared the same sort of work and lived the same sort of lives. As children, they might have been hired out to other farms, but as adults they seldom strayed far from home. The navvy rarely stayed anywhere long enough even to call it home. And if nothing else, farm life had a variety of jobs that changed with the seasons. There were seasons for ploughing and sowing and times for harvest, and there were the winter months that provided the opportunity to catch up on maintenance, relaying hedges, ditching and general repairs. The navvy's life had few such variations.

It might be thought that road building might offer similar opportunities to canal and railway construction, but the differences were crucial and lie at the root of the whole great transport revolution that began in the middle of the eighteenth century. Before that time, it would not be unfair to say that the state of the roads was a good deal worse than when the Romans had left Britain. There were many reasons for this. Wheeled vehicles were rare, but there was a huge movement of people and beasts, particularly the latter. Between 1776 and 1785 nearly a million beef cattle and almost 7 million sheep were driven on foot to Smithfield market in London.[6] It is not difficult to imagine the effect of all those animals on a badly maintained road, their hoofs churning the surface into a quagmire. Even the most important highways were neglected and in some regions decent roads were so rare that outsiders seldom took the trouble to even try to reach them. A writer in the *Gentleman's Magazine* in 1739 wrote that 'Dorchester is to us a terra incognito and the map makers might, if they pleased, fill the vacuities of Devon and Cornwall with forests, sands, elephants, savages and what they please'. Even when roads had a semblance of care taken over them, they were likely to be all but impassable throughout the winter months. The answer to this sorry state of affairs lay with the antique system in place for making and repairing them.

For centuries it had been the job of the individual parishes to take responsibility for the roads within their boundaries. To do the work they were allowed to call on the labour of villagers and required farmers to provide horses and carts. They were not paid, and not surprisingly no one was keen to do very much or indeed anything at all. Theoretically, magistrates could demand that the work was done and impose fines on parishes that failed in their duty. In practice, very little happened. Things began to change with the introduction of turnpike roads, where there was an incentive to provide something rather better than the general highway as those who used it were required to pay tolls for the privilege. The turnpike proprietors were required to pay the costs of building the roads, including labour costs, but once they were completed the duty of keeping them in good repair still fell on the parishes. There was little incentive to take road-building jobs, and none at all for having the task of repairing them. The end result was inevitable. The agriculturist Arthur Young described the roads he had known in the late eighteenth century:

> I remember the roads of Oxfordshire forty years ago, when they were in a condition formidable to the bones of all who travelled on wheels. The two great turnpikes which crossed the county by Witney and Chipping Norton, by Henley and Wycombe, were repaired in some places with stones as large as they could be brought from the quarry; and when broken, left so rough as to be calculate to dislocate, rather than exercise. At that period the cross roads were impassable but with real danger.[7]

Moving people and goods by road varied from being difficult to impossible and no one spent very much time building or retaining them. There was one area, however, where transport was becoming more reliable. Moving goods along navigable rivers was far easier and almost infinitely more efficient than moving them by land. And through the late seventeenth and early eighteenth centuries, river improvements were making the whole situation even better.

Rivers do not generally flow in the smooth regular fashion that would make them trouble-free as transport routes: sometimes they dash along furiously over rapids, and elsewhere they languish in shoals and shallows. More problems for boats wanting to use rivers were caused by the weirs built to divert water for use by millers. These same weirs did, however, help solve the problem of irregular flow. The water was always deep and calm above the weir, and consequently easy to navigate. All that was needed now was a means of getting boats over the top of it. This was accomplished with the flash lock. The weir was made up of moveable paddles. When they were lifted, the water was released in a sudden surge or flash – hence the name for this type of device. Boats could ride down the flash or be winched up against the stream. It was not the safest system; in 1634 a passenger boat with about sixty people on board overturned in Goring flash on the Thames. There were no survivors.

Even at the time of the Goring disaster, an alternative was available: the pound lock. This is the familiar lock, with a chamber closed by gates at either end. For a boat going downhill, the lock is filled with water until it reaches river level, then the top gates are opened and the boat passes in. The gates are then closed, and water drained out until it reaches the level of the lower river; the bottom gates are opened and the boat goes smoothly, and safely, on its way. This is obviously a far better system than the flash lock, but it requires more work to build. You cannot build a lock right across a river as it will simply act as a dam when not in use. The solution is to build a weir, and then divert the water down a side channel, just as the millers had always done to feed their waterwheels. The lock can then be built in this artificial cutting. The river engineers were, in effect, building a series of short canals with single locks to overcome differences in the levels of the natural river. These new, improved waterways were generally known as navigations, and we seem to have finally arrived at the first navigators. In a way we have, but we are still a long way from the professional navvy.

River improvement happened quite slowly. In 1600 there were approximately 670 miles of natural rivers in use, and just 60 miles of artificial cutting, making a total length of navigable river of 730 miles. By 1760, the length of natural river had reduced to 620 miles, but the engineered length had risen to 700 miles, almost doubling the available length of navigation.[8] That is a considerable achievement and involved a great deal of labour, but it was spread over a long time period – it works out at adding just 4 miles a year. No one was going to make a living working at that slow rate.

The year 1760 is significant. A time had been reached when river improvement could not be developed much further. The roads were still little better than they had been previously, but still large parts of the country had no access to water transport. And the country was just entering a period of immense industrial expansion, which depended on the movement of raw materials and finished products. There was only one solution: build wholly artificial canals to fill the gaps. Over the next seventy years the whole country would be covered by a network that would stretch for some 3,000 miles. The days of piecemeal changes were over. Now there was work that would not just last a few months, but would go on for years and even decades. The day of the professional navvy was about to arrive.

CHAPTER TWO

THE NAVVY ARRIVES

To understand how professional navvies became a vital force in canal construction, you first have to be aware of just how the whole canal age began in the first place.

River improvements had continued in a piecemeal manner up to the middle of the eighteenth century, and if the world at large had been more alert to what was going on, then the big change might have come a few years before 1760. In 1755 an Act was passed for the Sankey Navigation to join St Helen's to the Mersey. It attracted very little attention at the time, as the preamble referred to it as 'an Act for making navigable the River or Brook called Sankey Brook', which made it appear as no more than the latest in the series of river navigations. In fact, the brook did no more than supply what was in fact a wholly artificial canal. Its success might have started a general rush in canal building. As it was, nothing very much happened for the next five years. Then the young Duke of Bridgewater obtained his Act to build a canal to link the coal mines on his estate at Worsley to Manchester. This was unmistakably different, as the canal, far from making use of the nearest river, the Irwell, strode right across it on a massive stone aqueduct. It was one of the wonders of the age, and sightseers flocked to see the extraordinary sight of boats on the canal passing high over the tops of barges on the river. The canal became a stopping-off point for aristocratic tourists in search of the picturesque, but others were enthralled by a very different aspect of this modern marvel. Once it was open, the price of coal in Manchester was halved. Industrialists, especially those who had works in the Midlands remote from natural waterways, began to plan canals of their own. Within ten years a dozen Acts had been approved for a considerable network of waterways, serving the new industrial towns, such as Birmingham, and linking the four great rivers of England: Trent, Mersey, Thames and Severn. As well as the inter-connected network centred on the English Midlands, there were two major cross-country routes, the Leeds & Liverpool and the Forth & Clyde. The promoters were inspired by the Bridgewater, but it was not necessarily offering a model that could be applied everywhere.

The Bridgewater Canal was unique in many ways. For a start, it was paid for by a single individual, while the vast majority of later schemes were financed by forming companies and selling shares. The Duke also was able to rely in the first stages of planning on his very able agent, John Gilbert. Later they employed an engineer, a Derbyshire millwright, who had proved himself capable of handling problems involving water when he had taken on the job of draining the aptly named Wet Earth Colliery. His name was James Brindley. The workforce was employed directly, while on virtually all the later canals the work was let out to contractors, who had the responsibility of hiring and paying the workers. The success of the canal did, however, have far-reaching effects. Apart from encouraging others to take up construction, it made Brindley famous. He was the man everyone wanted as chief engineer. Historians are now inclined to give far more credit to Gilbert for the success of the Bridgewater, but whoever deserves the praise, it was Brindley who was available for work: Gilbert preferred to continue his well-paid employment with the Duke. The result was that the first generation of English canals tended to follow Brindley's ideas on the best methods of construction; and it was this first generation of canals that was to set the pattern for the future of much of the English canal system, though Scotland and Wales generally followed different paths.

Cutting a canal through level countryside is a comparatively straightforward business, but the British countryside is seldom level and those parts that are tend to be the ones where canals are least needed. The flat lands of East Anglia are ideal for agriculture, but the new industrial world tended to rely on water power to turn its machinery, and that often meant using reliable, fast-flowing hill streams. And there was one commodity above all others that provided a steady cargo for the boats – coal. It was the Duke of Bridgewater's considered view that the good canal had 'coal at the heel of it'. So if you wanted a profitable canal you had to go where the raw materials and their customers were – and that was not always in the sort of landscape an engineer would have chosen for an easy life.

Brindley faced precisely this dilemma on his early canals. His main concern when faced with obstacles was to go round them whenever possible, as a result of which many of the early canals wriggle snake-like across the land. But even Brindley's evasive tactics couldn't work everywhere. When he was faced with Harecastle Hill, stretching right across the line of his route for the Trent & Mersey as it passed through the Potteries, he had to face the fact that there was no way round: he would have to go through. He needed to build a tunnel. It is one thing to get men to dig a long ditch, quite another to produce a tunnel nearly 3,000 yards long. Brindley found the idea totally daunting. The Bridgewater had been built to take vessels almost 15ft wide, but the engineer baulked at the idea of building a tunnel that could accommodate them, so he decided to build it to take vessels half that width. He made life even easier for himself by deciding that the tunnel would not be wide enough to allow for either a towpath or for boats to pass each other. That, he thought, would be manageable and he boasted that it would all be finished in no time at all. He was wrong; it took eleven years to complete, and the engineer was dead before it was finally opened. As there seemed to be little point in building a canal to take broad vessels if they couldn't get through from one end of the waterway to the other, Brindley decided to design everything to take vessels of no more than 7ft 6in beam. Boat length was irrelevant as far as going through a tunnel was concerned, so locks and other features were designed to take boats the same length as those on the Bridgewater – and so the famous 70ft canal narrow boat came into existence. It reduced the amount of work needed everywhere: locks could be half the size of the ones at Runcorn, the canal itself needn't be as wide and consequently bridges would be smaller. It was a great saving in materials and work and set the pattern for canals throughout the English Midlands. Not everyone took the same line: a number of canals of the period, notably the Forth & Clyde in Scotland, the Leeds & Liverpool in northern England and the Stroudwater, Thames & Severn, were built with wide locks. But whatever the size of the canal an unprecedented amount of labour was needed, and many constructions continued for several years. The Leeds & Liverpool was begun in 1770 and, after numerous stops and starts, it was finally completed in 1816.

Following the completion of the first generation of canals, there was a lull in construction in the 1780s due to the trade depression caused by the American War of Independence. When the recovery came, the 1790s saw an explosion of canal building in what came to be known as the years of Canal Mania. Twenty-one new canals were begun in just one year – 1793 – at the heart of the mania. It was not just the number of canals that increased, but the work involved in building them changed as well. Where Brindley had gone round obstacles, the new generation of engineers – William Jessop, Thomas Telford and John Rennie – met them head on, driving through hills in deep cuttings and striding over valleys on embankments and aqueducts. The demand for skilled labour was immense, and a workforce had been steadily building up in the previous decades. It did not happen overnight.

Building a canal is a complex enterprise, requiring the skills of many craftsmen – bricklayers, stonemasons, carpenters and more. But at the heart of it is a long trench full of water, and that trench needs to be dug and that, in the eighteenth century, meant employing men with spades, pickaxes and barrows. The original Bridgewater Canal was not in fact very long at all, a mere 6½ miles, but it was built to take vessels up to 14ft 9in beam and over 4ft draught. As vessels using the canal travelled in both directions, the channel had to be large enough to allow them to pass each other along the way, and as they don't want to be scraping along the bottom, it needed to be dug to an appropriate depth. For the purposes of a very rough calculation, a reasonable estimate for the size of that trench on the Bridgewater would be 40ft wide and 6ft deep. A simple calculation of the area of the cross-section multiplied by the length shows that to dig this really quite modestly sized canal would involve removing approximately 300,000 cubic yards of soil, clay and stone. Later in the canal age, it was estimated that a strong professional navvy could shift 12 cubic yards a day.[1] It is unlikely that the men who dug the Bridgewater had built up the strength to do as much as their seasoned successors did, but let's give them the benefit of the doubt and say that every man averaged 10 cubic yards. They managed to get the job done in a year, so there must have been around a hundred diggers at work on this one short canal to get the work finished in that time. When you think that the next two canals begun after the success of the Bridgewater – the Trent & Mersey and the Staffs & Worcester – had a total length between them not of 6½ miles but of 140 miles, then you begin to get some idea of exactly why canal construction called for not a few workers, but a whole army of navvies.

The Duke of Bridgewater had few problems in finding a workforce: it was readily available in the form of estate workers and the miners of Worsley, but nothing in the contemporary records tells us a great deal about these men. Given the interest that was aroused by the construction of this pioneering waterway, one would hope to find something that would shed light on the issue. There are a number of accounts by travellers who visited the works, but sadly very little is to be learned from them. A typical example relates how the author watched the men at work for about two hours, and at the end of that the best he could manage was to describe the scene as being like 'the industry of bees, or labour of ants'. He commented how each man's work depended on co-ordination with the others, which is not very surprising, and ended with an even less helpful analogy: 'the whole posse appeared, as I conceive did that of the Tyrians, when they wanted houses to put their heads in, and were building Carthage'.[2] The author would have been secure in the knowledge that no one, including himself, had the least idea what Tyrian builders looked like, so he was safe from contradiction.

Following the success of the canal from Worsley, the Duke decided on an altogether bolder enterprise. The canal was to be extended by another 26 miles to join the Mersey at Runcorn, which would provide access to Liverpool. This involved building a set of locks to join the canal to the river, which would require an immense amount of masonry work. The famous potter, Josiah Wedgwood,

Between 1760 and 1831 Parliament passed 114 Acts approving canals in England, Scotland and Wales. Not all were actually constructed, but by 1840 an estimated 2,105 miles had been completed.

visited the site in June 1773 and described the construction as using blocks of stone up to 12 tons in weight. He noted that 'by the excellent Machinery made use of, some of which is still left standing, they had as perfect command of these huge Masses of Rock, as a common bricklayer has of the brick in his hand'. Sadly, there are no details of the machines or the men who did the work. Documents do suggest that the building of this extension involved a workforce of as many as 600 men, usually arranged in gangs of fifty, each with its own overseer. This was far more men than could be supplied entirely from the Duke's own employees, and workers were brought in from other areas, especially Yorkshire. Samuel Smiles, who wrote the biographies of several of the great engineers of the late eighteenth and early nineteenth centuries, did take the trouble to find out rather more about the actual people involved, though he seems to have believed they were all local. One has to remember he was relying on memories that were at best second-hand, for he was writing almost a century after the event. He did, however, have access to Brindley's notebooks, themselves fascinating documents which show that whatever his qualities as an engineer, he was scarcely literate. In his notes you can hear his Derbyshire accent, for he took his spelling from his own pronunciation, so 'bad luck' becomes 'bad louk' and an 'engine at work' is 'engon at woork':

> Brindley did not want for good men to carry out his plans. He found plenty of labourers in the neighbourhood accustomed to hard work, who speedily became expert excavators; and though there was at first a lack of skilled carpenters, blacksmiths, and bricklayers, they soon became trained into such under the vigilant eye of so able a master as Brindley was. We find him, in his notebook, often referring to the men by their names, or rather byenames; for in Lancashire proper names seem to have been little used at that time. 'Black David' was one of the foremen employed on difficult matters, and 'Bill o Toms' and 'Busick Jack' seem also to have been confidential workmen in their respective departments. We are informed by a gentleman of the neighbourhood that most of the labourers employed were of a superior class, and some of them were 'wise' or 'cunning men', blood-stoppers, herb-doctors, and planet-rulers, such as are still to be found in the neighbourhood of Manchester. Their very superstitions, says our informant, made them thinkers and calculators. The foreman bricklayer, for instance, as his son used afterwards to relate, always 'ruled the planets to find out the lucky days on which to commence any important work,' and he added, 'none of our work ever gave way'. The skilled men had their trade secrets, in which the unskilled were duly initiated – simple matters in themselves, but not without their uses.[3]

It is doubtful if a knowledge of astrology was of great use in canal construction, but this account does suggest that those who worked for the Duke and his agents were indeed out of the ordinary. One curiosity that Smiles noted – the use of nicknames – was very common among navvies and persisted through the years. There have been many reasons suggested for this, including the idea that a man might want to join the largely anonymous navvy army precisely because he wished or even needed to keep his true identity secret. Already one is beginning to see the first signs that the men who dug the canals were different from other workers. But we are still some distance away from recognising the professional navvy: it is probable that most of the men who came from the Bridgewater estates simply went back to their old jobs, if only because the Duke was known as a good and generous employer. So when did the navvy first appear?

Although canal companies generally kept careful records, many of which have survived, the contractors who did the actual hiring rarely did. Information about the first navvies is scarce and fragmentary, but it is still possible to build up, if not a complete picture, then at least a convincing sketch. In the early years, everyone was learning as they went along, and canal companies learned from each other. Work on the Coventry Canal began in 1768, two years after construction began on the Staffs & Worcester. Brindley was chief engineer for both projects, so he made arrangements for key figures from the former to make a trip to see how things were done. One of the clerks was seconded from the Coventry for three weeks and a carpenter was sent over to see how lock gates were made. Even the most commonplace objects were copied: 'Resolved that one hundred wheelbarrows be provided and that an advertisement be published for Persons to undertake the making thereof according to the Model lately sent from Staffordshire.'[4]

Everything about canal construction was new and that included the manual work. Not surprisingly, once the canal companies had got teams of men at work who had gained the necessary strength and skill to do the job properly, they wanted to keep them. In the early days, contracts had to be let out to whoever was willing to take them, and those who took on the work had to train up the men they employed. But to ensure they kept at the work once they were competent, these men were legally bound by contracts. However, in a rapidly changing world there was always the temptation to cash in on skills that were in demand. In June 1767 a contractor on the Staffs & Worcester put an advert in a Birmingham paper giving a list of men who had absconded with brief descriptions and the heights of each, and threatening legal action against any other contractor who employed them.[5] It was not just the men themselves sloping off to look for better pay, the canal companies were not above indulging in a little poaching as well. In 1768 the Birmingham Canal Company noted that some of their stone cutters had been enticed away with the offer of better wages. The Chesterfield Canal Company tried to prevent such things happening on their sites by passing a regulation that specified if anyone did run away they would be brought back and the cost of doing so would be deducted from the miscreant's wages. Clearly canal work was in a state of flux, and the worker who had become accustomed to the hard labour of the diggings was highly valued. The day of the professional navvy was dawning.

In 1788 the Reverend Stebbing Shaw paid a visit to the workings on the Basingstoke Canal, where work was starting on the 1,200-yard-long Greywell Tunnel:

> I ... saw about 100 men at work, preparing a wide passage for the approach to the mouth, but they had not entered the hill. The morning was remarkably fine, 'The pale descending year, yet pleasing still', and such an assembly of these sons of labour greatly enlivened the scene. The contractor, agreeable to the request of the company of proprietors, gives the preference to all the natives who are desirous of this work, but such is the power of use over nature, that while the industrious poor are by all their efforts incapable of earning a sustenance, those who are brought from similar works, cheerfully obtain a comfortable support.[6]

The message could scarcely be clearer: the professional navvy had arrived. As the number of canals under construction grew, so the demand for labour, and especially skilled labour, increased. Canal companies could no longer rely on recruiting local workers. In July 1776 the Stroudwater company had to send a man north to try to find suitable labourers, and the following month he was able to report that he had 'engaged a considerable number of men in Warwickshire and Leicestershire'.[7]

The other interesting point in Shaw's notes is the fact that the local poor weren't able to earn enough from canal work. This obviously means that they were not being paid a wage, but were being paid by piecework. This was an inevitable part of the system, as contracts were generally let out at so much per cubic yard of canal dug. The going rate in the early years seems to have been fairly steady at 3d a cubic yard. The contractor would need to take his profit, so the men would get less than that. It was only the very best, work-toughened navvies who could dig 12 cubic yards, which would earn the contractor three shillings, of which the navvy might not get more than two shillings for himself. But what of the poor local man who might only be able to do half as much work – he was only making a shilling a day. Rates for navvies increased quite dramatically over the years. By 1793 the Lancaster recorded having 'from 230 to 250' men at work at 2s 6d a day. That was among the highest rate recorded, and rates did tend to fluctuate with demand and availability of labour. The figures alone don't mean much unless they can be seen in terms of earnings elsewhere and the cost of living.

It is notoriously difficult to get any idea of earnings in general for eighteenth-century Britain. There were enormous regional variations, especially among agricultural workers, and there are many different factors to take into account. An agricultural worker with a cottage would normally expect to have a patch of land on which to grow a few vegetables that would help keep the family. And there were seldom any fixed rates: farm workers were paid less in winter than in spring, but would expect a big boost in earnings at harvest time. In Oxfordshire at the beginning of the nineteenth century, the average wages for men were 9s 6d a week in winter, 11s 6d in spring and 19s a week at harvest time, but they would have been a good deal lower fifty years earlier. The figures do at least suggest that the wages paid to navvies at this time were comparable to the highest rates paid on farms during the short harvest period, and well above those paid during the rest of the year. A more direct comparison for the 1790s can be made, which gives more of an indication of average pay in the farming community. When the JPs of Speenhamland in Berkshire met in 1795 to work out the minimum sum that a family could live on, they came up with 6s a week for a man and wife; anyone earning below that would have their pay made up by the parish. These men were not being generous: this was mere subsistence level. It is not difficult to see why a farm worker could not immediately make a living in canal work and why they might be reluctant to give up the comforts of home to go away to work. It is also clear that those who built up the strength and skill, men who had no family ties, would think very differently.

There were others who would consider canal work to be well worth their trouble. Ireland was notorious for the poverty of many rural areas. An early nineteenth-century Parliamentary Report on conditions described families living in huts with sod roofs, with practically no furniture, not even beds to sleep in, and existing on a diet virtually entirely of potatoes. There was a tradition of the Irish coming over to England at harvest time. Passage was cheap if you weren't too fussy. In 1779 a cabin cost £1 1s, but if you were prepared to sleep in the hold it was just 2s 6d, and you could make that up in a good day on the farm. There is a tradition that most of the navvies came from Ireland, but very little actual evidence to support it. Nevertheless, when the Caledonian Canal was being constructed, with one of its prime aims being to provide employment for the Scottish Highlanders, the chief engineer Telford had difficulty convincing the committee that he was indeed using Highlanders and not Irish. As a patriotic Scot himself, he was more than a little indignant at the suggestion. In the end,

There were estimated to be over 2,000 Scots and Irish working in the Edinburgh area in the early 1840s. While the Scots were able to get accommodation, the Irish had to make do with wooden huts erected by the contractor. The huts were approximately 20ft by 10ft, and filled with tiers of bunk beds with usually two or three to a bed. They held anything from twenty to thirty people, and that could include wives and children.

the appeal of canal work was easy to explain. Telford and Jessop had to write annual reports on progress on the Caledonian, and they made the position perfectly clear:

> As canal work is very laborious, they must give such Wages ... as will be the means of procuring and calling forth the utmost exertions of able Workmen; so that although the Wages paid by the Contractors may be higher than for common Workmen, yet when compared with the quantity of Work performed, it is by much the cheaper labour.[8]

That is it in a nutshell: the professional navvy was paid more because he had to work harder to earn it. For the man prepared to do that it was a way of life that gave him a better living than he could expect doing anything else. There was a price to pay. He had to abandon any idea of a settled life and tramp the country looking for the best deal he could get – and he was not likely to feel any loyalty to any employer. This did not make life easy for the harassed canal engineer, anxious to get work done: there was always the possibility of men being lured away, which is what happened on the Kennet & Avon:

> The works on the upper Level go on slowly principally owing to the Men being enticed to leave the works by greater advantage being held out to them by a Contractor at Bristol. But I have some expectations that some of them will return after finding their Disappointment. The Consequence will be that the Contractor must pay higher wages.[9]

High wages were good news for the workers, but bad news for other employers, particularly farmers. Sir Charles Morgan tried to bring a Bill to Parliament to 'restrain the employment of labourers in the time of the corn harvest'. It met with stern opposition from MPs who could see no reason why Parliament should interfere in the matter. In the age of laissez-faire economics it was generally accepted that it was up to employers to get workers at whatever wage they could and if farmers wanted to keep their men on the land then it was up to them to pay the price. Others pointed out that many who worked on the canals had never done anything else, so it made no sense to try and force them to work on the harvest:

> Mr. Dent was against the bill in question: he said there were hundreds of people who came from Scotland and from Ireland, for the purpose only of working in canals, and who knew nothing of corn harvest. If this bill passed, they would be entirely deprived of the only honest means they had of subsistence.[10]

The Bill was defeated. In practice it was not uncommon for navvies to leave the workings at harvest time if the farmer was offering good enough money.

And there were canal companies who bowed to the inevitable. In 1793 the Ashby Canal's engineer was told to reduce the workforce to let men go to the harvest 'for the good of the country'; and the following year work on the Peak Forest Canal was delayed until the harvest was in. By this time, at the heart of the mania years, the demand for labour was at its peak and contractors and canal companies were advertising widely to attract workers. Never had so many canal navvies been at work at the same time, but what exactly did they do and what were their lives really like?

CHAPTER THREE

THE NAVVY LIFE

Basically it might seem that all the navvy had to do was dig a very long ditch. So he did, but that was only a part of the work. When a canal was dug through porous soil it had to be made watertight by 'puddling'. A full description was given in an instruction manual of 1805:

> Puddle is a mass of earth reduced to a semifluid state by working and chopping it about with a spade, while water just in the proper quantity is applied, until the mass is rendered homogeneous, and so much condensed, that water cannot afterwards pass through it, or but very slowly. The best puddling stuff is rather a lightish loam, with a mixture of coarse sand and gravel in it: very strong clay is unfit for it, on account of the great quantity of water which it will hold, and its disposition to shrink and crack as this escapes.[1]

The puddle was spread to at least 18in thick at the bottom of the canal, and then covered with a layer of soil. It needed to be 3ft thick on the sloping sides to prevent water getting through and damaging the banks. The best way of ensuring that the puddle was firmly and evenly kept in place was by stomping on it, and special heavy puddling boots were used. It was a thankless task, stamping up and down on a heavy, cloying mixture, and worse still when there was no extra pay for doing it. Puddling was often included in the basic rate for cutting. Sometimes, however, suitable puddling material wasn't available locally. On the Kennet & Avon in 1804, John Rennie, the chief engineer, discovered that the nearest source was so far away that he instructed the men to construct a tramway – an early form of railway on which horses hauled the trucks – from the clay pits to the canal. There was so much work involved that a new contractor had to be called in just to complete a mile of puddling. Some canals created far more trouble than others. The Thames & Severn begun in 1780 was notorious for its leaks and called for extreme measures to try to keep it watertight. The canal company followed the normal practice of letting out the work to contractors, which in reality meant anyone who could get a gang of men together. John Pickston was simply described as 'a cutter', which probably meant he had been a navvy on another canal and had brought some of his old workmates with him. He was given the important job of puddling one of the worst sections. The engineer's specification called for a double lining. First there was to be a 2ft-thick layer of puddle, and above that another 2ft of trodden clay, known as 'pun'. The work had to be done carefully – laying a thin layer, working it, letting it dry for a day or two and then adding the next layer, and so on. Pickston was paid by results not by the day, so he must have thought no one would notice if the bottom layer of puddle was thin, so long as the pun on top was thick enough. But the shortcomings became all too obvious when the water was let in. The engineer was furious and wrote an angry letter to Pickston, listing the failings and ending: 'As you wish to be called a workman <u>read and blush</u>.'

In the Brindley days, cutting the canal was comparatively straightforward thanks to his practice of following the natural contours of the land. Later canals were very different, and the new, direct approach often involved going through low hills in deep cuttings. This inevitably made for harder work, as the men were soon through the easily removed topsoil and into heavy clay or even rock. When rock was reached, the usual solution was to drill holes, pack them with gunpowder and blast the rock away. This was a time before power drills or safety fuses, so the drilling all had to be done by hand, and judging the explosions called for a nicety of judgement. On many canals the evidence of drilling and blasting is still to be seen, like on a deep cutting on the Barnsley Canal where huge stone blocks have been tumbled down the cutting side. Excavating a deep cutting produced a new problem: how to get the spoil out of the cutting. The answer was the barrow runs. Planks on trestles were laid up the side of the cutting, ropes were attached to the barrows and were hauled up by horses using rope wrapped round a pulley. The navvy had to wheel the barrow to the foot of the run, and then attach the rope and set off up the planks, balancing the barrow in front of him. It is not hard to imagine the difficulty of balancing a loaded barrow while trying to keep your feet on sloping planks, smeared with mud and clay. If a man slipped he had to try and throw himself to one side of the plank and the load to the other, to avoid arriving at the foot of the slope with the barrow on top of him. Coming down again was no less precarious, as the man ran down with the barrow behind him. The broadsheet ballad *The Navigators* describes the scene:

> Now when that we come to the bottom run,
> We fill our barrows right up to our chin,
> We fill up the barrows, right up, breast high,
> And if you can't wheel it, another will try.

And when that we come to the main plank wheel,
We lower our hands and stick fast on our heels;
For if the plank does bend or go,
Our ganger on top cries, 'Look out below'.

Robert Southey, who was to become poet laureate, was a friend of Thomas Telford's and went with him to see the work in progress on the Caledonian Canal. He visited Laggan where a short neck of land had to be cut through to join Lochs Oich and Lochy, and here a rather more sophisticated system was in operation:

Here the excavations are at what they call 'deep cutting', this being the highest ground on the line, the Oich flowing to the East, the Lochy to the Western Sea ... The earth is removed by horses walking along the bench of the Canal, and drawing the laden cartlets up one inclined plane, while the emptied ones, which are connected with them by a chain passing over pullies, are let down another. This was going on in numberless places, and such a mess of earth had been thrown up both sides along the whole line, that the men appeared in the proportion of emmets on an ant-hill, amid their own work. The hour of rest for men and horses is announced by blowing a horn; and so well have the horses learnt to measure time by their excursions and sense of fatigue, that if the signal be delayed five minutes, they stop of their own account without it.[2]

Digging deep cuttings was only one aspect of the new style of engineering directness. Often the spoil from the cuts was carted or boated away to build up an embankment over the next valley, the whole process known as 'cut and fill'. This might seem to offer fewer problems and less hard work for the navvy, but it was a process fraught with danger. The banks could become very unstable and sudden collapses and landslips were common, especially after heavy rain. The most spectacular examples of cut and fill are to be found on what is now the main line of the Shropshire Union, but both cuttings and banks suffered greatly from slips during construction. None proved more difficult than the embankment at Shelmore that came to be known simply as The Great Bank. By 1831 there were between 300 and 400 men on the site, and about seventy horses hauling the cartloads of spoil. The more the men piled on the soil, the more the bank slipped. Telford decided he was using the wrong sort of soil, and he brought in different material from another part of the workings. The result was the same. All kinds of different methods were tried until the bank was finally stabilised in 1835. Similar problems occurred on other canals, and represented a real danger to the navvies. Accidents occasionally got reported in the local press: 'Early on Saturday morning last, a little beyond Winson Green, in the Birmingham Canal Navigation, the Earth fell suddenly in and killed John Lester, one of the workmen occasioned, it is thought, by the heavy Rains on Friday Evening.'[3]

Other features that occur at regular intervals throughout most canals are the locks. The chambers all had to be dug out and there is rather more work involved than might appear. A typical lock on a narrow canal might be listed as having a rise of 6ft and able to take a vessel 7ft 6in beam. But the chamber had to be wide enough for the vessel to get into the chamber with water to either side, and initially it would have to be dug even wider to allow walls of brick or stone to be built. A fall of 6ft does not mean that is the depth to be dug. There had to be a lining on the bottom. There needed to be sufficient water below the boat at the lower level to keep it afloat and the water never reached the brim. A reasonable estimate of the size of a chamber would be at least 10ft across, 10ft deep and 80ft long. So one is looking at getting on for 100 cubic yards to be dug out. Broad canals would need at least twice as much. On an extreme example, like the Rochdale Canal with eighty-nine broad locks in just 33 miles, lock digging represented a major part of the whole construction programme.

The most spectacular canal structures are the aqueducts and even here the ordinary navvy had a role. The immense stone aqueduct that carries the Lancaster Canal across the River Lune has five semicircular arches, each spanning 70ft. Work began in January 1794 and fortunately the man in charge, Archibald Millar, sent regular and detailed reports back on progress at the site, which give one of the clearest pictures we have of what exactly went on during a major undertaking. Millar had an assistant, Exley, who had risen up through the ranks to reach the position of assistant engineer, for which he received a salary of £250 a year; he had the help of a foreman, a former carpenter, 'a person of integrity' who was given what was considered a handsome salary: '18 or 20/– a week certain would be a very pretty inducement to a good working man.' This was to be a site that would be teeming with workers within a few weeks. The canal had to be brought to a level for the river crossing, but the aqueduct itself demanded a huge amount of manpower. Because piers would have to be constructed on the river bed, coffer dams needed to be built and the space inside them had to be kept as dry as possible. This involved pumping out the space inside the dams using a primitive steam engine. Once that was done, foundations were constructed by driving piles of specially imported hard Russian timber into the bed. This work was expected to last a long time. Exley was provided with temporary accommodation on site, which he had to share with the foreman. Millar's instructions set out that Exley was:

to erect a shade, proposing it to cover a Saw Pitt, a Carpenters Shop, a room & kitchen for himself & a Store room. The kitchen will serve the Steam Engine man also. These buildings I have desired to be enclosed with the Slabs, that will come off the Foundation frame & Piling: And the posts to be made of the inferior Balks that may be unfit to be used under the Masonry. I have desired that the room for Exley to sleep in may be floored, and that it, with the Kitchen and

Store Room be separated with Slabs, and that a fire place be made in Exley's room & in the kitchen also.

His final comment seems almost superfluous given his description of a home made up of the odds and ends on the site that weren't fit to be used for construction: 'I have designed them to be raised on the most frugal Plan.'[4] Aside from sharing his hut with the foreman, which could hardly have been a comfortable situation, the engine man who shared the kitchen was frequently drunk and was eventually sacked. Reading this description of the accommodation for one of the senior men on site, one cannot help but wonder where the rest of the workforce stayed. There were a lot of them to find homes for: by June there were 150 at work around the aqueduct.

Piling was the worst job, not helped by atrocious conditions. The whole site was flooded more than once, and on one occasion the living quarters were submerged. Another time, the coffer dams were breached and planks, piles and even wheelbarrows were swept away by the floodwater. When work was possible, the men were toiling away in deep, cloying mud as the steam engine worked rather ineffectually to keep everything dry. It was wretched work, and Millar suggested the men needed encouragement: 'a little Beer will be necessary given to the Workmen to stimulate exertions'. It was dangerous, too:

> A labourer at the Lune Aqueduct had the misfortune yesterday to have three of his Fingers on the right hand taken off by the Piling Ram falling upon them. I should recommend him to the attention of the Committee to give him a small sum to assist him in his present situation.[5]

The Lune aqueduct was at the heart of a massive operation and on the canal as a whole in 1794 there were roughly 1,000 men at work, while over 200 horses and carts were in use to carry materials. But of all the works carried out along canals, none gave more problems to engineers and men than the construction of tunnels.

Brindley had done all he could to minimise the work needed to construct Harecastle Tunnel on the Trent & Mersey by reducing its size as far as he could. The one thing he could not reduce was its length, and at almost 3,000 yards it was an immense undertaking. It was added to the Barton aqueduct as an interesting spot on the new tourist map of Britain, though there must have been precious little to see at the surface. Nevertheless, one enthusiastic visitor described it as 'the eighth wonder of the world' and declared that Brindley 'handles rocks as easily as you would plumb-pies'.[6] The same account included one interesting detail that the tunnel contained 'a stove, the fire of which sucks through a pipe the damps that would annoy the men, who are cutting towards the centre of the hill'. As the tunnel was cut in part through coal measures, the 'damps' could have done more than annoy the men: they could kill them.

There were two damps: fire damp, which was methane and explosive; and choke damp or carbon dioxide that suffocated. The treatment suggests the latter and this was a common treatment in mines; the fire at the bottom of the shaft would have been disastrous if methane had been present.

The problem faced by the eighteenth-century engineers was compounded by the fact that the science of geology did not exist at the time, so no one knew what to expect when work began. At Harecastle the tunnellers met everything from solid rock that had to be blasted away to soft material that was virtually quicksand, so that as fast as it was dug out more seeped back in again. The water- and wind-powered pumps that had been used at first proved hopelessly inadequate and a steam engine had to be brought in to help. Much of the tunnel had to be lined, and the bricks had to be made on site out of local clay. Each brick was put together by hand in a mould, and the clay had to be worked really hard to get rid of any air bubbles. It was not unlike preparing puddle. Given the problems and the pioneering nature of the work, eleven years no longer seems an amazingly long time for completing the job.

Brindley was a pioneer, but the engineers who followed him did not necessarily fare any better, and the men who had to do the digging and blasting did not find things any easier either. Sapperton Tunnel on the Thames & Severn was on an altogether grander scale than Harecastle: 3,817 yards long but, more importantly, built to take barges up to 11ft beam. Once again, the workers met a variety of material along the way from oolitic limestone to fuller's earth. Building a tunnel is not a straightforward business of starting at one end and continuing until you arrive at the other. Once the line had been determined, workers started from both ends, and in between shafts were sunk down to tunnel level. There were twenty-five of them altogether on the Sapperton, and once they were sunk men could descend and work out from the bottom of the shaft in both directions. Each shaft was roughly 8ft in diameter and the job of getting the spoil out usually relied on a horse gin, a simple device where a horse walked round a circular track to turn a windlass. Men went up and down in the bucket or basket. Night and day had no significance down in the dark workings of the tunnel so men worked in shifts. It has been estimated that as many as 300 were employed.

The work was dangerous. The various gins were insecure, and down in the darkness lit only by candles, the gloom was made even worse by the regular explosions as the rock was blasted away. Temporary rails were laid in the workings to carry solid-wheeled trucks moving the

Of all the works carried out along canals, none gave more problems to engineers and men than the construction of tunnels: at Harecastle the tunnellers met everything from solid rock that had to be blasted away to soft material that was virtually quicksand.

spoil. There were usually gangs of eight men working out from the foot of each of the shafts, each with their own specific jobs: the miners worked at the face, hacking and blasting; the loaders filled the carts; and other men manhandled the loaded carts to the foot of the shaft and brought back the empties. Accidents were inevitable, but no one kept a very accurate account of them. It was notable that the number of deaths recorded in the village of Coates, at one end of the tunnel, doubled during the years of construction. The *Gloucester Journal* for 22 January 1787 recorded one incident among many:

> In the prosecution of this work, many men have lost their lives; one man was killed a few days ago by the carelessness of his companion, who suffered one of the boxes used for drawing the earth up the shafts to fall down into the pit, which killed the person at the bottom. The men were brothers.[7]

One consolation for this hard-pressed workforce was that they had somewhere reasonable to live at the Coates end of the tunnel. The New Inn was a three-storey building specially constructed for the purpose. There was a tap room, where the men ate and drank, and two floors above which were simply open dormitories. As one shift got up for the day or night's work, another shift fell into the beds they had left. When work was completed the New Inn was used by the boatmen on the canal, and it is still there today, but minus its top storey and renamed The Tunnel House. The Bricklayers Arms, now the Daneway Arms, at the other end of the tunnel probably got used in much the same way.

Work went on reasonably quickly, after a slow start under the management of an incompetent and probably dishonest contractor. By 1788 the work was virtually complete and in the course of the job the men used roughly 800 barrels of gunpowder for blasting and burned an estimated 4,000lb of candles to light the work. Not surprisingly, with the smoke from all those candles and the dust and smoke from blasting, a similar sort of ventilation system had to be used to that employed in the Harecastle.

Britain's longest canal tunnel took the Huddersfield Narrow Canal under Standedge Fell, the Pennine hill that separates Yorkshire from Lancashire. It is 5,415 yards long and took longer to complete than any other – an astounding sixteen years. This was not so much due to the difficulty of the task as the fact that the company kept running out of money, but it did mean the workforce were on site for a very long time. The moorland under which the tunnel passes rises to over 1,000ft and is bleak, treeless and uninviting, yet it is here that navvies and their families made their temporary homes. Walking across the moor one can still find the remains of old construction shafts, many left as ventilation shafts, surrounded by spoil. Here, too, are the foundations of buildings that mark where the shanty towns of shacks and rough cottages grew up. Anyone who has ever ventured up here in winter will know just what a hostile environment it is and how tough it must have been for the families. As at Sapperton, there are suggestions in the records of men killed in the workings, roughly fifty or so. They were mostly from the north of England and some may have been brought in because of previous experience in mining. John Kell, who died in March 1810 for example, came from Stanhope in Weardale in the heart of lead-mining country.[8] The records also show an increase in infant mortality during the construction period, suggesting that many navvies had their families with them and the babies were unable to survive the harsh conditions on Standedge Fell.

One aspect of canal construction can easily be overlooked: the reservoirs. Canals need a water supply. When a lock is filled, the water comes from the pound, the expanse of water above the lock. When it is emptied, the water passes on down to the next pound and can be used for the next lock lower down the system, and so on. But when you come to the summit level, there is no lock above to draw on, and unless the summit is kept supplied it will simply dry up. In the case of the Rochdale Canal, one of the three trans-Pennine routes, the summit level is high in the hills and the only way to keep it in water was to build reservoirs. Eventually seven reservoirs were built, all clustered around Blackstone Edge, but to get an idea of the work involved it is worth concentrating on the biggest, Hollingsworth, now regarded as a beauty spot and known as Hollingsworth Lake. It covers an area of over 100 acres and holds 400 million gallons of water. Digging that out was a monumental task and so was constructing the immense earth bank that forms the dam. It was built with a 1:2 slope, with a 9ft-thick core of puddle clay to keep it watertight. The top of the bank was made to a width of 10ft so that it could take a road-way. The amount of work needed to keep the Rochdale Canal in water must have been comparable to the work required to build the waterway itself.

The conditions under which navvies lived and worked varied immensely from one canal to the next, and depended also to a large degree on their employer. The vast majority were directly answerable to the contractors who employed them. As mentioned earlier, the gangs under the control of a contractor could be anything from half a dozen to several hundred men. Sometimes a small consortium would be formed. One of these which took work on the Brecon & Abergavenny Canal consisted of William Watkins, labourer, Thomas Powell, shopkeeper, and William Parry, gentleman. It is a fair guess that these were local men, with Watkins providing the muscle, Powell the equipment and Parry the cash – and possibly an air of respectability. Contractors did not need, however, to be local at all. When work started on the Lancaster Canal, the company put adverts in the papers of all the major towns between Edinburgh and London. The value of a contract might be quite small. On the Oxford Canal, John Watts was paid £350 a mile for cutting the canal through Lord Craven's estate – and unless it was an exceptionally large estate, that probably did not amount to very much. But the man who did a good job and was careful with his money might move on to greater things. Hugh McIntosh was born in Scotland in 1768 and after a perfunctory education got himself taken on as a navvy on the Forth & Clyde Canal. By the 1790s he had managed to acquire a small contract with the Lancaster Canal, but by 1823 he was describing himself as a Contractor for Public Works with an office in Bloomsbury Square, London. That year he was awarded a contract for completing the Gloucester & Berkeley Canal worth £111,493 15s 11d. Sadly, he got an eye infection while working on this contract, which left him blind, but did not stop him from working as a contractor through into the railway age. He was proof that a navvy could become rich – even if very few actually did.

Although the advantages of contracting out work were obvious, it took some time to work out the best way of organising it. The Coventry Canal was among the first to be started and when work began in 1768 contracts were given out on the basis of labour costs alone, the company agreeing to provide all the equipment. This meant that a gang of navvies could be formed without any need for finding the capital to pay for essentials such as tools and wheelbarrows. The problem soon became clear. As the contractors did not own the equipment they didn't have to be responsible for it, so the company ended up paying men just to look after the hundred wheelbarrows they had bought at a cost of 7s each. Then they had to pay someone else to gather them all up when a section was completed and move them on to where they were needed next. Even then things went missing, and they had to advertise to try and get them back: 'Ordered that an advertisement be published in Hand Bills and in the Coventry News Paper offering a Reward of Five Guineas for the Discovery of any Person who has stolen any of the Rails belonging to the Company or taken away Wheelbarrows or other Utensils.'[9] The company having given out contracts still tried to keep things under their own control. 'Ordered that Mr. Wheeler do superintend the Labourers … and take check at proper times of their Numbers and he is impowered to discharge any of them who are negligent.'[10] Eventually they realised that they were getting the worst of both worlds: not having direct control of the workforce but paying out money to oversee it and look after their assets. Soon the system was changed. Contractors were obliged to find their own equipment and to take responsibility for the men they employed. The navvies were totally dependent on the

> Conflicts occurred throughout the construction process. The company wanted to get the work done as cheaply as possible and would often award the contract to the lowest bidder. The contractor then wanted to start the job as quickly as he could to receive his payments. The resident engineer and the company secretary wanted the work done thoroughly and to perfection, even if it took longer.

contractors and had no direct link with the company. This meant, for example, that the company would not take any responsibility for accidents, though some were prepared to make small payments to help out.

There was one fundamental problem with the whole system. Contractors were paid according to the amount of work they completed and it was in their interest to get it done as quickly as possible. The company wanted work to be done as thoroughly as possible, and were not too concerned about how long it took. There were excellent contractors who appreciated that doing a thorough job earned them a reputation that would ensure future work. Others were more interested in short-term gains. The partnership of John Pinkerton and John Murray took on a major part of the work on the Lancaster Canal, which meant that they had several hundred men under their direct control. At first all seemed to be going well, but troubles soon appeared. Murray wanted to get started on as much of the canal as possible, without worrying too much about completely finishing off one section before moving on to another. It kept his men fully occupied and brought payments closer. The company was not impressed:

> Mr Murray is wanting to begin upon the New Lot, but the Come have refused to give him liberty at present because he may employ a greater number of Men on the present Lot. & the Land for the New Lot is not agreed for. The Come have great complaints that the work is not finished off as they go along, and a number of more hands might be employed without rambling over the Country & creating Damage unnecessarily.[11]

The complaints continued of work skimped and orders ignored. In their rush to get ahead the contractors apparently subcontracted some of the work, including masonry, to groups of navvies who had no experience in these fields, but were happy to pocket the extra pay. On this occasion the men profited from the system, but there were other times when they were the losers. Pinkerton and Murray needed to be sure that there were always enough men available to do the work as it came along, and if that meant that at times the navvies and subcontractors were idle and therefore unpaid, that was unfortunate but, as far as they were concerned, necessary. The men complained to the company, but although the company was always ready to get involved with issues that directly affected the progress of work, it had no intention of siding with the navvies in a disagreement with their employers. It was a three-way contest between the company, contractors and navvies – one in which the navvies seldom won. Sometimes they won a partial victory. In 1798, men who had not been paid asked the company to sort things out for them, but were turned down. Again, the company did not want to interfere. But there was some very urgent work that needed to be done, so the navvies working on that section got their money.

The one time of the year when the navvies were in a strong position was during harvesting. Farmers offered good pay to lure men away, and neither threats nor promises could bring them back. This was the situation round the Lune aqueduct in the summer of 1794:

> On Saturday last Mr Cartwright endeavoured all that he could to have all the Carpenters & Labourers at work, flattering them with Encouragement of Beer on the one side and threatening those who did not come should have no more Employment at the Aqueduct. The Scots men, Particularly the Carpenters, paid no respect.

But the Lancaster Canal company secretary, Archibald Millar, knew time was on his side. He ended his report by noting: 'I hope and expect a little time will correct these combinations. The Harvest will not last always.'[12]

Problems over pay were an ever-present part of the canal construction period. The contractors needed to get the money from the company and the men needed to get theirs from the contractors. Things could easily go wrong. The Oxford Canal Company obviously expected trouble on pay day in 1770 when they 'ordered that 2 Pairs of Pistols be purchased --- to be delivered into the hands of the paymaster to this Company for the use of the Company's Agents'.[13] Far greater problems arose when the company itself ran out of funds, which happened on the Huddersfield Narrow Canal, where they were reduced at one point to only paying bills of less than £30, and paying everyone else five shillings in the pound. As the biggest debts were owed to contractors, the misery was passed on down the line. Even when there was money available, there was often a problem in finding the actual coins: there were simply not enough in circulation. John Pinkerton solved this problem to his own satisfaction by paying the navvies working on the Basingstoke Canal in tokens. The 1s tokens had a picture of a sailing barge and the words Basingstoke Canal on one side and a wheelbarrow with pick and shovel, the name John Pinkerton and the words 'one shilling' on the other. This system of issuing trade tokens was common in many industries at the time. Local tradesmen were told that if they accepted the tokens in payment from the workers, they could be exchanged for coin of the realm when presented to the employers. This was an inconvenience that not all tradesmen were prepared to accept. In practice, the concern that had issued the coins often set up their own stores. This was good business for men like Pinkerton who, having made a profit from the work of the men, now made a second profit when they spent their wages. There are few details of how this token system worked on the canals, but we shall meet it again when we turn to railway construction. Another method of payment was to give the men twenty-one day notes, rather like cheques, which they then had to get cashed at discount and so had to pay for the privilege of getting their own money.

When the men felt they were being cheated or had trouble getting cash, there was more than a possibility that real trouble would follow. At Sampford Peverell on the Grand Western Canal, that was exactly what happened. The men had a grievance, the sense of injustice was fuelled by drink and the end result was a riot:

> A number of the workmen, employed in excavating the bed of the Grand Western Canal, assembled at Wellington, for the purpose of obtaining change for the payment of their wages, which there has been lately considerable difficulty in procuring. Many of them indulged in inordinate drinking and committed various excesses at Tiverton, and other places, to which they had gone for the purpose above stated. On Monday the fair at Sampford seemed to afford a welcome opportunity for the gratification of their tumultuary disposition. Much rioting took place in the course of the day, and toward evening a body of these men consisting of not less than three hundred, had assembled in the village. Mr Chave (whose name we had occasion to mention in unravelling the imposture respecting the Sampford ghost) was met on the road and recognized by some of the party. Opprobrious language was applied to him, but whether on that subject or not, we have not been informed. The rioters followed him to the house, the windows of which they broke; and, apprehensive of further violence, Mr Chave considered it necessary to his defence to discharge a loaded pistol at the assailants. This unfortunately took effect, and one man fell dead on the spot. A pistol was also fired by a person within the house, which so severely wounded another man, that his life is despaired of. A carter, employed by Mr Chave, was most dreadfully beaten by the mob. Additional members were accumulating when our accounts were sent off, and we understand their determination was to pull down the house.[14]

The 'ghost' was a man paid by Chave to rattle chains and moan on his property, and accounts vary from one version that claimed it was to frighten away an unwanted tenant, to another that it was a con to trick people into paying for visits to the 'haunted house'.

It is not too surprising, given this and similar accounts, that the arrival of navvies to an area was not always welcomed. Anyone visiting Sampford Peverell today will find a small, quiet village and one can easily imagine the sense of alarm among the locals when 300 rough, tough, boozy strangers arrived in the district. You can also see why so many were needed, because the canal near the village is carried on a huge embankment that must have represented a great deal of labour. Very little effort seems to have been made to welcome the newcomers, either here or anywhere else. One Lancashire vicar did invite navvies to a welcoming sermon, though any who turned up must have been less than enthralled by hearing themselves described as men who habitually 'cheat, and steal, and drink, and swear, and fight, and do all kinds of mischief to themselves and others'.[15] The reputation of the navvies was so widespread that it seems that on at least one occasion they found a way of increasing their earnings by acting as a hired mob to intimidate voters. One of the engineers on the Lancaster Canal had to explain to the committee why work had come to a halt:

> We are going on very ill with work in this neighbourhood, not a man has been at work since the Canvassing began & I doubt it will be the case as long as the election continues, Lord Stanley's party having hired them, which can be for no other purposes than to riot and do mischief.[16]

One can easily get the impression that the navvies were as fearsome and as prone to rioting as such accounts suggest. An obvious source for information about the navvies, apart from official canal records, is the press of the time. Looking through the papers for areas in which canal work was going on, certainly the impression you come away with is that there were more days spent rioting than working. But then one has to remember that newspapers print news. They do not print stories saying that several hundred men worked hard and peacefully in the area this week; they do report when things go badly wrong. It is easy to get things out of perspective. There is also the question of provocation. The arrival of a comparatively well-paid body of men with money to spend on food and drink encouraged too many unscrupulous businessmen to raise their prices. This happened to the workers on the Leeds & Liverpool Canal:

> The Labourers for cutting the canal are much imposed on by extravagant charges of the Inn keepers and the Committee are desired to consider if any scheme can be come into for the convenience of such Labourers by erecting tents, Booths, &c &c providing them with meat & drink at a more easy expence.[17]

In the event the company did nothing: ultimately the navvies were left to fend for themselves. When they did take matters into their own hands, things could quickly get out of control and rapidly developed into a general riot, fuelled by drink. That is exactly what happened among the navvies working on the Witham Navigation in 1812. Here the men had a specific problem with the local baker who supplied their bread and a more general grievance about inflated prices charged by other suppliers, including innkeepers. Protest soon turned into a fully fledged riot. They called at The Plough pub, where they removed the landlord and drank his beer, and then went on to the baker's where they pelted him with his own bread before moving on to a second pub, The Bottle and Glass, which they attacked and rolled out the beer barrels. The landlord of a third pub, The Angel, didn't even wait for them to attack – he rolled the beer out and locked himself indoors. Things then got even nastier:

During the time they invested the houses in Bardney, the people were so frightened that they gave them anything they asked for: the navvies went about to the inhabitants of the village demanding money and different articles from them, and proclaiming their own prices for provisions for the future.[18]

Eventually the Riot Act was read, the cavalry moved in and 'in due course these disturbers were prosecuted and imprisoned'. If they suffered no more than imprisonment they were comparatively lucky: the harsh laws of the time allowed judges to give rioters the death penalty.

It is also necessary to see navvy riots in the context of the age. It was a time when working people often felt under threat and could look for little help from the law. One could choose from various examples drawn from many industries. The work of the framework knitters of Nottinghamshire was covered by a set of laws, which included regulations on what work could be done by apprentices and what was the preserve of qualified journeymen. Employers flouted the rules and in 1778 the workers took their case to Parliament: 'Some boys, who are Paupers, are put to work at the age of ten or eleven, but they make bad work of it – That the work affects their nerves very much … the masters of these boys make them work till Eleven or Twelve o'clock at Night.'[19] This was illegal but Parliament refused to act. The men who had gone to put their case were sacked on their return to Nottingham, and things got worse. In another section of the textile industry, the Glasgow weavers won a court case to be paid the minimum agreed wage, but the employers did nothing and simply ignored the judgement. The weavers went on strike and at last the law took an interest – the strike leaders were sent to prison. It is against this background of authority seeming always to take the side of the employers that action became violent. In Nottingham a secret army of aggrieved framework knitters began smashing the machines of employers who flouted the law. Their leader was a mythical character, General Ludd. Machine breaking and Luddism has come to be thought of as mindless opposition to mechanisation and progress, but the machines the Nottingham Luddites were breaking had been in use for over a century without any trouble. It was the last resort of desperate people who had been failed by the law and who decided that violence was the only answer. In many histories the Luddites are cast as villains or simply misguided, but to many local people they were heroes, as a broadsheet ballad of the day made clear:

> No more chant your old rhymes about bold Robin Hood
> His feats I do little admire.
> I'll sing the achievements of general Ludd,
> Now the hero of Nottinghamshire.
> Brave Ludd was to measures of violence unused
> Till his sufferings became so severe,

That at last to defend his own interests he roused,
And for the great fight did prepare.[20]

This is the context in which the navvy riots have to be seen. This is not to con-
done the violence, which all too often affected those who had little or no interest
in the navvies or their lives and had never been involved with them in any way.
But it does perhaps make clear that they were not alone in what they did, and
countless other stories can be told of riots in many different communities.

Some riots, however, had no obvious cause apart from the fact that those
involved were drunk. The workers on the Carlisle Canal, described as mostly
Irish, went on the rampage in the 1820s:

> During the whole of Sunday last, the neighbourhood of Caldew bridge was dis-
> turbed, and passengers disturbed by a number of these persons, who, not content
> with excessive drinking and fighting in the streets, proceeded to plunder the
> tavern-keepers of their property. One party took forcible possession of the Fox
> and Grapes Public-House and plundered the place of spirits, ales &c.[21]

If they were not actually stealing their booze, men were willing to buy illegal
hooch smuggled in from Ireland. Things didn't always work out as expected.
A group of the Carlisle navvies paid for their liquor by persuading the smug-
gler that the tradesman's bill they were giving him was a £10 note. They must
have thought it was a brilliant idea as they enjoyed their free drink, but it
turned out to be not such a bargain after all. The moonshine liquor was a
lethal brew that killed off five of the navvies.

Many of the problems arose from poor accommodation and the lack of
supplies at reasonable prices, including drink. Unfortunately, detailed records
of how the navvies lived are sparse for the canals, simply because no one
recorded them. The one exception is the Caledonian Canal where, because
it was being paid for by the government, reports of progress had to be made
on a regular basis. During the second year, the report gave details of living
conditions:

> The accommodation and markets near the intended Canal, and especially at the
> South-West End of it, are so little adequate to the wants of a numerous body of
> Workmen and Labourers, that we have found it necessary to continue our atten-
> tion to their habitations and subsistence; temporary Sheds and Huts for lodging
> most of the Labourers have therefore been erected; and we have continued in
> some degree the supply of Oat meal at prime cost … With a further view to the
> welfare of the Persons employed, We have encouraged the establishment of a
> small Brewery at Corpach, that the Workmen may be induced to relinquish the
> pernicious habit of drinking Whiskey; and cows are kept at the same place to
> supply them with Milk on reasonable terms.[22]

Future reports failed to disclose whether the Highlanders who made up the vast majority of the navvy force were ever persuaded to exchange their drams for glasses of beer, let alone milk. The huts and sheds seem to have been quite crude, but they were not free – the men paid rent for sleeping in them. Later, as permanent structures such as cottages and stables were built, they were occupied – but the ones who got the stables had to share them with the horses used in the workings. It was a Spartan life in rough and ready accommodation, and the men mostly had to make do with a diet of potatoes and porridge. But the Caledonian may not have been typical of canal workings in general. The Highlanders who took the work had been desperate, often dispossessed of their simple crofts by the big landowners who were taking more and more of the country. Regular meals, a roof over their heads and a reasonable rate of pay must have been an unlooked-for blessing. In England and Wales, where work was more plentiful, men had to be tempted to take canal work by above average wages, but that does not mean that living conditions were any better than they were on the Scottish diggings. The canal navvy's life was a hard one – hard work and hard living – and whatever they got they definitely earned.

Towards the end of the canal construction period, the practical limits of the work were being reached. This was particularly true in the industrial region of South Wales, where canals could only be built in the valleys while many of the mines and works they served were up in the hills. The answer was to construct tramways, simple railways set on stone sleeper blocks, leaving a space between the rails for a horse to walk, hauling trucks along the line from mines, quarries and ironworks to the waterway. The Brecon & Abergavenny Canal is only 33 miles long, but it was served by no fewer than fourteen tramways, with a total length far greater than that of the canal itself. Altogether, over 1,000 miles of tramway were constructed in the canal age. The advantages of the system are obvious: it meant, for example, that the ironworks at Blaenavon, high in the hills, could send its pig iron down to the canal and then eventually onwards by water all the way to Cardiff. Not everyone was so sure they were a good thing, however. The Duke of Bridgewater famously remarked that canals would do well enough if only they could keep clear of 'those damn'd tramroads'. His suspicions were to prove well founded.

The iron masters of Merthyr Tydfil had co-operated to promote the Glamorganshire Canal, but when it was opened in 1794 co-operation gave way to rivalry. The canal was a victim of its success and the northern end, between Merthyr and Abercynon, was particularly badly affected by congestion, with boats queuing to use the locks. Matters were made worse when Richard Crawshay of the

The Bridgewater Canal was unique in that it was financed by a single individual, while the vast majority of later schemes were financed by forming companies and selling shares.

Cyfarthfa ironworks, who had a majority of the shares, demanded that his boats got preference. Samuel Homfray of the Penydarren ironworks decided to solve the problem by building a tramway from his works to Abercynon, bypassing the blockages. It would have remained a tramway no different from any other in South Wales if Homfray had not written to a young Cornish engineer in 1803 inviting him to bring his newly invented machine to the tramway. The engineer was Richard Trevithick and his machine was a steam locomotive. In February 1804 the engine made its first run down the tracks, and the canals had a rival. Many canal navvies were about to find they had a new role in life: no longer digging canals but building railways.

CHAPTER FOUR

THE RAILWAY AGE BEGINS

Richard Trevithick's pioneering locomotive was a success, in that it did what was required of it, as Samuel Homfray who had arranged the experiment in the first place was delighted to record:

> I have the satisfaction to inform you the Tram Road Engine goes off very well – we have made a journey on our Tram Road 9½ miles in length – it took 10 Tons long wts of iron & about 60 or 70 people riding on the Trams which added 4 or 5 tons more to the wt – it goes very easy 4 miles an hour, & is as tractable as a Horse, will *back* its load, & move it forwards as little (& slow) as you please.[1]

What Homfray did not mention was that the heavy engine had an unfortunate tendency to crack and break the brittle cast-iron rails. Homfray kept the locomotive, but mostly set it to work as a stationary engine powering machinery at the ironworks. Another Trevithick engine, sent to the colliery district of north-east England, failed for exactly the same reason. Trevithick made one last attempt to interest the world at large in his invention by running a new locomotive, called 'Catch-me-who-Can', which was built for speed as much as for haulage of heavy loads. It ran on a circular track in London and visitors were charged a shilling a time for a ride behind the engine that advertised 'Mechanical Power Subduing Animal Speed'. It attracted a lot of attention, but no one came forward to put money into developing the locomotive as part of a proper railway system. Discouraged, Trevithick accepted an order for stationary engines to pump dry a silver mine in Peru; he left Britain to oversee their erection and did not return until 1827. He was forgotten and so too, for many years, was his steam locomotive.

The return of the locomotive was largely brought about as the result of the very different ambitions of a Frenchman. When Napoleon went to war against Britain there was an economic crisis and the price of fodder for horses rose alarmingly. The owners of a colliery at Middleton, near Leeds, took their coal to the Aire & Calder Navigation by tramway. Concerned about the increasing costs, the colliery agent John Blenkinsop began thinking about steam power. He was aware of Trevithick's problem with broken rails and he thought of an ingenious way to overcome it. He would build a light locomotive and increase traction by using a cogged wheel on the locomotive to engage with a toothed rail laid alongside the conventional rails – the rack and pinion system now seen only in mountain railways. He was not a mechanical engineer, so he turned to Matthew Murray, a successful Leeds engineer, to convert his ideas into a practical system. A link with Trevithick remained, in that they had to pay for the use of his patent. In June 1812 the system went into service with two engines and the world's first successful commercial railway was in business.

Inevitably the colliery owners of north-east England took an interest, as many of them relied on tramways connecting their mines to the two main rivers, Tyne and Wear. William Hedley of Wylam Colliery was the first in the field, and he was able to introduce modifications to the locomotive that enabled it to run without having to use the cumbersome rack and pinion system of Blenkinsop and Murray. Killingworth Colliery was the next to acquire an engine. They had a young and ambitious engineer working for them and the owners sent him over to the Middleton Railway to see how their engines had been designed. His name was George Stephenson. His first locomotive *Bluther*, which borrowed several ideas from the Murray engine, was set to work in the autumn of 1813. For the next few years railway development was concentrated in the north-east, but there was no attempt to do anything beyond running them on the tramways that were already in place, simply replacing horses with locomotives to pull the trucks. As far as the navvies were concerned, transport construction still meant building canals and Acts for new waterways were still being passed right up to the 1820s, including two canals that were notable for their heavy earthworks: the Macclesfield and the Birmingham & Liverpool Junction. Thomas Telford, the leading canal engineer of the day, was well aware of the development of steam locomotives, but he believed that their use should be restricted to working on tramways, feeding material into navigable waterways. Others had different ideas, notably George Stephenson.

Developments among the collieries of Northumberland meant that those further south in Durham, served by the Tees, were being left behind. As early as 1810 a meeting had been called in Stockton-on-Tees to discuss the possibility of building a tramway or canal from there to Darlington. Eminent engineers were consulted, but nothing much happened until 1821 when a prominent industrialist from Darlington, Edward Pease, took an interest. There are various accounts of what happened next. Samuel Smiles, who always liked a romantic story, told how the young Stephenson, describing himself as 'only the engine-wright at Killingworth', arrived unannounced on Pease's doorstep to persuade him to abandon his plans for a horse-drawn tramway in favour of a steam railway. This is unlikely as Stephenson by then had a considerable local reputation and was not noted for his modesty. A more realistic version came from another engineer, Nicholas Wood, who actually accompanied Stephenson on the visit to Pease. He described how they took the coach from Newcastle to Stockton and then walked the 12 miles to Darlington to get an idea of the country through which the proposed line would pass. They then went to see Pease by appointment.

Stephenson was not the only one putting forward ideas for the new line. George Overton, who had been the engineer responsible for the Penydarren tramway, had already drawn up plans for a conventional tramway, one in which horses did the work and wagons would have smooth wheels, running on a plateway, where the rails were L-shaped and the vertical flange would keep the wheels in place. Stephenson proposed a railway to be worked by steam locomotives, with flanged wheels running on edge rails. Stephenson won the argument and was appointed chief engineer. He wrote initially to Murray to ask if he could supply locomotives, but the latter declined, explaining that they had not built any locomotives for many years. Stephenson had little option: he would have to design and build the engines himself, with the help of his son Robert. They set up Robert Stephenson & Company in Newcastle-upon-Tyne.

The Stockton & Darlington Railway was in many ways quite unlike anything that had gone before. The earlier colliery lines had all been based on previously existing tramways and plateways, and were in effect private lines. The Stockton & Darlington was approved by an Act of Parliament, passed in April 1821, but which still left the true nature of the line undecided, merely specifying 'a Railway or Tramroad'. This was to be the first public railway. Its planning, however, was still in the tramway tradition, and in laying out the line and planning the engineering features Stephenson took his cue from the canal engineers. The route varied as a canal route would have done between contour cutting and earthworks. The main difference came when there were large changes of level to be negotiated. Where a canal would have had locks, the railway had inclined planes that used stationary steam engines to haul the trains of wagons up and down the slope by cable. There were, nevertheless, a number of important innovations on the line. Stephenson had entered into a partnership with William Losh to produce cast-iron rails, but when he heard that John Birkinshaw had taken out a patent for rolling wrought-iron rails, with an I-shaped cross-section, he at once realised their superiority and ordered them for the line. The problem of broken rails now had a permanent solution, to everyone's delight except William Losh, whose cast-iron rail business was made instantly obsolete.

In some ways the tasks facing the navvies were not dissimilar to those confronting the canal builders: tunnels to be forced through the hills, cuttings to be dug and banks to be built. There was, however, a new task to be learned: rails had to be laid. The track was formed as tramways had been for some time, with rails that came in 15ft lengths, fastened to stone blocks. The blocks had to be squared off and then drilled to take a wooden plug. When the rail was set on top of the block, a spike was driven through a hole in the flange of the rail and into the plug. The system was designed to leave a clear path between the rails for horses to walk. Manhandling rails and driving spikes was to become a familiar part of the navvy working life. Stephenson was joined in the work by his son Robert, and they set about recruiting some of the workforce themselves, including George's two brothers, James and John. The rest of the work went to contractors, who employed mostly local men. The railway engineers soon found they faced problems that were all too familiar to their canal counterparts. Thomas Storey, a former mining engineer and now one of the two resident engineers on the project, wrote to Pease describing the antics of one of the subcontractors:

> J. Hastings has been making another break up of the wagons and carrying away walls by running them *amain* which might as easily [have] been houses. The destruction of the Co's property by this sub-contractor has not been less than 50 or 60£. He refuses to carry on the work any way but that of his own, deposits the earth where and how he pleases, and runs the risks of lives and Property by wilfully running the waggons at improper speed down the inclines and across the turnpike at Auckland. John Stephenson wishes to be clear of him and has therefore for that purpose given the cut up.[2]

There were few real engineering problems, though there was some difficulty in a very boggy area, known as Myers Flat. Stephenson's solution was to keep piling earth along the line of the track until it stopped sinking and a firm foundation had been created. But in the process, as the earth settled, it pushed away the marshy land and as it moved it took the line of fences with it. This apparently totally bewildered the navvies who, faced with a fence that moved in the night, decided it was the work of fairies.

In spite of difficulties with contractors and bog fairies, the line was opened on 27 September 1825 and huge crowds turned out to see the first locomotives draw coaches full of dignitaries down the line. It was, however, the last time that passengers would be taken by steam power on the Stockton & Darlington for some time. I have a poster on my study wall advertising the passenger service offered by 'the Company's Coach called the Experiment', which ran every day except Sunday between Stockton and Darlington and back again. It was exactly what the name suggests, a stagecoach specially fitted with flanged wheels and pulled by horses. Passengers paid a shilling for a one-way trip and were allowed to take parcels of up to 14lb free of charge. To us it seems an anachronism, but one has to remember that although this was a public railway, its main function was little different to that of the old tramways. It was there to take coal to the Tees. That was why it attracted such little interest and excitement in the country as a whole; it might have had a different title but in practice it was to most people just another of those colliery lines. It did, however, encourage the promotion of a much more ambitious plan, for what would be the world's first intercity railway, to link Manchester and Liverpool. It represented the decisive moment in railway history and its inception had a close parallel to the birth of the canal age.

The Act for the Liverpool & Manchester Railway was only approved after fierce opposition from the various waterways that would be affected, including the Bridgewater Canal. There is more than a touch of irony in the fact that the Duke of Bridgewater had been opposed by the older river navigation companies, and now the Bridgewater Canal was lined up with the old enemies against the railway supporters. On both occasions, the old brigade prophesied the doom of their enterprises if the newcomer was allowed to appear in the world. The Act was duly approved, however, after acrimonious wrangles, in May 1826. One vital question still remained to be answered. The Act still referred to the line as being 'a Railway or Tramroad' and in spite of the success of the Stockton & Darlington, there were many who were not convinced of the value of the steam locomotive. George Stephenson was still a passionate supporter of it, but there was a powerful faction among the promoters who favoured a very different system. They wanted to see a relay of stationary engines established along the line, which would haul the carriages and wagons along from one engine to the next. The question that needed to be decided was this: can a locomotive do the job of pulling trains over such a long distance and at a good speed? The answer was to hold a trial for an engine that 'must be capable of drawing after it, day by day, on a well-constructed Railway, on a level plane, a Train of Carriages of the gross weight of Twenty Tons, including the Tender and Water Tank, at the rate of Ten Miles per hour, with a pressure of steam in the boiler not exceeding Fifty Pounds on the square inch'.[3] The test took place on the line at Rainhill in 1829 and was famously won by *Rocket*, designed by Robert Stephenson.

This is not a book about locomotives, but there is a curious coincidence connected with the event that is worth telling, as it brings us right back to that first locomotive trial in 1804. Robert Stephenson had, like Trevithick, gone to South America with the idea of making a fortune in the local mines. He received an urgent message from Newcastle to return home to design the new locomotive for the trial. Meanwhile, Trevithick had been fortunate enough to find gold in South America but, realising that he needed to get

Navvies working on the Basingstoke Canal were paid in tokens. The 1s tokens had a picture of a sailing barge and the words 'Basingstoke Canal' on one side and a wheelbarrow with pick and shovel, the name John Pinkerton and the words 'one shilling' on the other.

the ore from the mines in the mountains to the coast, he set off with companions to try to find the best possible route, through difficult and unmapped
country. After many misadventures, he arrived at Cartagena, having lost most
of his possessions en route and unable to pay for his passage to England. And
there, also waiting for a passage home, was Robert Stephenson. There is no
record of what they talked about, but surely they must have discussed steam
locomotives and one would like to think that Trevithick mentioned how he
had managed to increase the heat in the firebox of his engine, by turning the
exhaust steam from the cylinder up the chimney, dragging extra air through
the fire. This was one of the key innovations that made *Rocket* a model for
future developments. Whether as a thank you or just out of his own good
nature, Stephenson loaned the older engineer enough money to book his
passage back to England.

In the meantime, work on constructing the line was going ahead. One
would have expected the company to recognise that after more than half a
century of canal construction the best system for employing labour had already
been worked out. But Stephenson was never a man to follow others' advice
and, in spite of having already worked on the Stockton & Darlington, he had
little experience of civil engineering. So he decided to go back to the old
system of employing direct labour. Altogether some 600 men were employed,
but only sixty of them it seems came from Durham or Northumberland, areas
that had the greatest experience of railway construction. There is no record
of how many were recruited from the ranks of the canal navvies. What we do
know is that the organisation seems to have been somewhat shambolic. The
company had arranged for an Exchequer loan of £10,000, but before making
the money available they called for a report from the eminent engineer
Thomas Telford. He sent an assistant, James Mills, to look at the works. Telford
must have been astonished by the report describing what he had found:

> There does not appear to be a single contract existing on the whole line.
> Stevenson [sic] seems to be contractor for the whole and to employ all the dif-
> ferent people at such prices as he thinks proper to give them, the Company
> *finding all materials*, not only rails and wagons but even *wheelbarrows* and planks
> etc. there is some difficulty in making out the value of what is to do … the
> first men I asked as to price said: 'I have no fixed price or specified distance to
> take the stuff (spoil); Mr. S. gives 8 pence, 10 pence or 13 pence as he thinks it
> deserves.' I asked him how far he was to do the cutting, he said nothing was
> fixed, he might go 20 yards further or half a mile.[4]

Mills seemed almost incensed by what he discovered as he visited the three
different districts where work was going on under the supervision of three
resident engineers.

Each has 200 day men employed and pay them every fortnight as *Company's* men for laying temporary roads, moving planks, making wheelbarrows, driving piles, and, in short, doing *every thing* but putting the stuff into the carts and barrows which is done by a set of men which is also under their direction and to whom they pay 3½d per yard to 5s as they think it deserves.

The system was clearly far from ideal, but the work went ahead at a reasonable rate despite the fact that there were a number of major engineering problems faced during the construction of the line.

Chat Moss was an area of peat bog covering 12 square miles, which according to local tradition was bottomless. It wasn't, but in places there was a layer of oozy, black mud to a depth of 20ft before hard clay was reached. It was a treacherous place, and the navvies who worked there followed the example of the local farmers and tied planks to their feet to spread the load and stop themselves sinking. Planks were also laid as pathways above the ooze, but when one of Stephenson's assistants, John Dixon, paid his first visit to the swamp he slipped. He was disappearing into the bog when the navvies rushed to pull him out. Stephenson had no option: he had to build his line across the area. He began by trying to dig drainage ditches and history repeated itself. Just as when Brindley had tried to do the same thing when constructing the Bridgewater Canal, as fast as a ditch was dug, the mud oozed back in. Whether Stephenson was told about Brindley's solution or not, he did exactly as his predecessor had done more than half a century earlier: as each section of trench was dug, he created a pipe out of rows of barrels set end to end, with their tops and bottoms knocked out. He then tried to get a solid foundation by trying the technique he had successfully used at Myers Flat. He brought cartloads of soil and tipped them on to the land, but they were no sooner tipped than they began to sink and soon disappeared from sight. Stephenson found one solution in the bog itself, when he noticed that coarse plants were bound together and appeared to float like rafts on the surface. He ordered the men to pile on brushwood and heather to create artificial rafts that were stable enough to take the loads of earth. It did not always work, and in some places he had no option but to keep on tipping. Stephenson himself recalled that he despaired at times: 'We went on filling in without the slightest apparent effect. Even my assistants began to feel uneasy and to doubt the success of the scheme. The directors, too, spoke of it as a hopeless task, and at length they became seriously alarmed.' Eventually, a rudimentary bank emerged above the level of the bog and a 5ft-high embankment crossed Chat Moss.

The Edge Hill Tunnel at the Liverpool end of the line was the next major undertaking. It was to be over a mile long, but represented far more work than a canal tunnel of the same length. It had to be wide enough to take a double track with rails set 4ft 8½in apart – which was eventually to become the standard gauge for Britain – and high enough to take the locomotives with their tall chimneys. At the peak of construction some 300 men were at work and the system of organisation was based on that of the canals, with shafts being sunk and headings worked out from the bottom, but not it seems with any great accuracy. Some of the shafts were so far out of line that side tunnels had to be dug at right angles to the correct line before any forward progress could be made. Henry Booth, the company's treasurer, described how some of the men had to be forced back into the works because of alarming earth and rock falls and the threat of flooding. The dangers were very real, as the local paper reported:

> We are pained to state that a labourer, who was working in the excavation of the rail-road at Edgehill, where the tunnel is intended to come out and join the surface of the ground, was killed on Monday last. The poor fellow was in the act of undermining a heavy head of clay, fourteen or fifteen feet high, when the mass fell upon him, and literally crushed his bowels out of his body.[5]

He was the first navvy to be killed in constructing a railway tunnel, but by no means the last.

If the scale of the tunnel was far greater than anything attempted in the canal age, then so too was the cutting at Olive Mount on the approach to Liverpool. It stretched for 2 miles and had to be hacked out of sandstone to a depth of 70ft. Contemporary prints show it looking more like some natural gorge than any man-made cutting. It must have been mightily impressive, but is rather less so today as it was later widened to take four tracks. There was one other feature that today shows the impact that the arrival of this new transport system had on its predecessor. The pioneering Sankey Brook was crossed by an elegant viaduct carried on nine arches, each of 50ft span. They stand some 60ft above the canal to allow sailing barges to pass underneath. But no sailing barges or indeed boats of any kind come this way any longer, and what was once a canal is now no more than an indentation in the ground, filled in long ago.

The opening of the Liverpool & Manchester on 15 September 1830 excited a huge amount of interest, with the Duke of Wellington, still a national hero as the victor of Waterloo, being the chief guest. It was not the civil engineering that created a stir, but the novel sight of steam locomotives travelling at previously undreamed-of speeds. It was probably the speed that caused the death of the local Member of Parliament William Huskisson, who strolled out of his carriage, failed to get off the track in time and was run down by *Rocket*. His death cast a blight over the day, but did nothing to dampen the general enthusiasm for rail travel that followed the opening. This was something new and

The Gangs Act of 1867 contained a range of measures including the banning of employment of children under the age of eight.

wonderfully exciting: no one had ever travelled at such speeds before, for engines were now capable of reaching 30mph. The brilliant young actress Fanny Kemble, the star celebrity of the age, was given a footplate ride with George Stephenson himself at the regulator. Her account captures the thrill of the experience:

> You can't imagine how strange it was to be journeying on thus, without any visible cause of progress other than the magical machine, with its flying white breath and rhythmical, unvarying pace, between these rocky walls, which are already clothed with moss and ferns and grasses; and when I reflect that these great masses of stone had been cut asunder to allow our passage thus far below the surface of the earth, I felt as if no fairy tale was ever half so wonderful as what I saw.[6]

The Liverpool & Manchester was quite different from all the earlier lines. They had all been built for freight with passengers as something of an afterthought. But this was a genuine intercity line. The passengers were hauled by steam, not by horses, and had specially built stations in which to buy their tickets and wait for their trains. No one in the early years had foreseen that passenger traffic would become a vital part of a new rail system, but it was soon apparent that this was exactly what was happening. Men began to dream of a time when not just cities, but towns and even villages would be linked by iron rails. Just as the construction of the Bridgewater Canal had opened the way to a huge expansion of canal building, now the country was gripped by railway mania. The experienced canal navvies would be sure of work stretching far into the future, and far more men would be joining their ranks to meet the insatiable demands of the railway builders.

CHAPTER FIVE

THE RAILWAY NAVVY

There is a great deal more information available about the railway navvy than there is about the canal navvy, and we also get more hints about how, where and why they were recruited. Documents about life in the country in the nineteenth century are also more revealing than those for the eighteenth century, and they make it clear that the system we think of as typifying the work of the navvy, with groups of men being led by a ganger who had the responsibility of dealing with the contractors about pay and conditions, were not unique after all. One of these workers described in his own words the system that was used to hire workers to bring in the harvest:

> I daresay you've heard of the 'lord', as we used to call 'im? Sometimes he was the horseman on the farm, but he might be anybody. His job was to act as a sort of foreman to the team of reapers – there was often as many as a dozen of us – and he looked after the hours and wages and such-like. He set the pace, too. His first man was sometimes called the 'lady'. Well, when harvest was gettin' close, the 'lord' 'ld call his team together and goo an' argue it out with the farmer. They'd run all over all the fields that had got to be harvested and wukk it out at so much the acre. If same as there was a field badly laid with the weather, of course the 'lord' would ask a higher price for that. 'Now there's Penny Fields', he'd say – or maybe Gilbert's Field – or whatever it was; 'that's laid somethin' terrible', he'd say. 'What about that, farmer?' And when the price was named he would talk it over with his team to see whether they'd agree. The argument was washed down with plenty of beer, like as not drunk out of little ol' bullocks' horns; and when it was all finished, and the price accepted all round, 'Now I'll bind you', the farmer 'ld say, and give each man a shilling.[1]

The gang system was particularly common in East Anglia, and was not limited to harvesting. It spread to other local activities, including digging the drainage ditches and dykes that were essential for turning the fens into usable agricultural land. These gangs who turned up wherever they were needed were viewed with something of the suspicion that became attached to any itinerant group, including the navvies. The conditions under which they worked were so poor that the government eventually stepped in. The Gangs Act of 1867 contained a range of measures including the banning of employment of children under the age of eight. It is not difficult to imagine that railway work would be no less appealing to some of these groups.

Public opinion took little notice of the canal navvies, but the arrival of the railways attracted more attention. Commentators began to write articles about them and where they came from:

Hodge [a farm labourer], deep-chested and broad-backed, discovers by association and comparison that if he can eat as much meat and drink as much beer as the stranger, he can do nearly as much work, so he sacrifices those parish ties so dear to the ignorant and timid peasant, and takes to the shovel and the wheelbarrow.[2]

Thomas Brassey, one of the greatest of all railway contractors, was one of those who started by employing as many former canal navvies as possible, but eventually had to recruit from farm workers. According to his biography, he found that Hodge was in reality 'but an indifferent specimen of a labourer when he first commences, and he earns only about two shillings a-day. Gradually he acquires some of the skill of his fellow-workmen; and then he rises into a higher class, receiving three shillings a-day.'[3] For everyone prepared to look at the work the navvies did, there were many more who were only concerned with their morality – or lack of it. Sometimes it seemed that any stick would do to beat the navvies with. One commentator on navvy life claimed that they were brutes simply because they used nicknames, or, as he called them, 'barbarous epithets'. It was, indeed, a very common practice. Some men kept their nicknames wherever they worked; others were assigned nicknames because of some quirk of behaviour on a particular site. There was an amazing array of names handed out or chosen by navvies. Often they did no more than reflect their origins – Brummagem or Bristol Jacks – but others defied definition. Who could explain the names recorded on the Kettering and Manton line: Skeedicks, Moonraker, Concertina Cockney, Fatbuck, Scandalous, Rainbow Ratty and many more? It was all tied to the navvies' establishment of their own identity, and it extended to their talk between them-

Thomas Brassey worked as a contractor in fifteen different countries, including Britain. Nine of them were in Europe; the others were Syria, Persia, India, Canada, Argentine and Australia. The rates paid to local workers varied from 4½d a day in parts of India to 7s a day in Australia.

selves, which had a close relationship to cockney rhyming slang. When a navvy announced that he was off on 'the frog and toad', a clergyman solemnly pronounced that 'the motion of the two reptiles is suggestive, I suppose, of a man on the tramp'.

Taking nicknames and adopting their own language was the least of their sins. John Francis wrote a diatribe against them, in which it seemed the most heinous crime they committed was poaching: 'game disappeared from the most sacred preserves.'[4] It is an interesting use of the word 'sacred', but to a Victorian the violation of the property rights of a country gentleman ranked on a par with highway robbery and not far behind murder. Poaching was just part of the way of life of the navvy, but according to Francis things got far worse once they started drinking:

> Like dogs released from a week's confinement, they ran about and did not know what to do with themselves. They defied the law; broke open prisons; released their comrades, and slew policemen. The Scotch fought with the Irish, and the Irish attacked the Scotch; while the rural peace-officers, utterly inadequate to suppress the tumult, stood calmly by and waited the result.

Having expressed his own opinion he brought in the Church to reinforce it:

> The 'navigators', wanderers on the face of the earth, owning no tie and fearing no law; 'were' said the Rev. St. George Sargent, 'the most neglected and spiritually destitute people I ever met; ignorant of Bible religion and Gospel truth, infected with infidelity, and prone to revolutionary principles'.

The Reverend St George Sargent had, in fact, been appointed as a chaplain on the Lancaster & Carlisle, his stipend paid by a benefactor anxious to bring religious belief and acceptable behaviour to the men. He appears to have conspicuously failed and when he was questioned in Parliament about his work, he described the navvies as socialists on the rather dubious grounds that they lived with women who were not their legal wives and 'doubt the authority of the word of God'. Yet he still managed to sell 350 Bibles to the ungodly socialists. The navvies had their own argument for not being convinced by the preachers. Thomas Jenour, who was a lay reader working for the Pastoral Aid Society on the Croydon & Epsom Railway, noted that they 'have expressed astonishment that God should have made some rich, and some so dreadfully poor'. He does not record how successful he was in convincing them that spiritual matters were infinitely more important than mere money. The most common view of the navvies among the clergy was much closer to that of Sargent, who could find little if anything good to say about them. One of the clergy was particularly shocked to discover that after he had given away Bibles, the navvies sold them to buy booze.

If the navvy really was deep-chested, broad-backed Hodge looking for a better way of life, how had he fallen so quickly into such a state of infamy? Or were the navvies really a special breed of men, coming from a wide variety of backgrounds? One man who painted a different picture from those already quoted was Samuel Smiles. When he was writing about the workers on the Bridgewater Canal he had to rely on second-hand accounts for his information. It was a very different matter when it came to railways. He first met George Stephenson in 1840, was greatly impressed by him and was later to write his biography. He was also enthused by the whole idea of railway construction and by 1845 he was himself employed as assistant secretary to the Leeds & Thirsk Railway, which was then still in the planning stage. He was to remain associated with the company for over twenty years, and therefore was actively involved throughout the whole period of construction. It is this direct involvement with the work that makes his account of the railway navvy about as reliable as one could expect to find and is consequently worth quoting at length:

The 'railway navvies' as they were called, were men drawn by the attraction of good wages from all parts of the kingdom; and they were ready for any sort of hard work. Many of the labourers employed on the Liverpool line were Irish, others were from the Northumberland and Durham railways, where they had been accustomed to similar work; and some of the best came from the fen districts of Lincoln and Cambridge where they had been trained to execute works of excavation and embankment. These old practitioners formed the nucleus of a skilled manipulation and aptitude, which rendered them of indispensable utility in the immense undertakings of the period. Their expertness in all sorts of earthwork, in embanking, boring, and well-sinking – their practical knowledge of the nature of soils and rocks, the tenacity of clays, and the porosity of certain stratifications – were very great; and, rough-looking as they were, many of them were as important in their own department as the contractor or the engineer.

During the railway-making period the navvy wandered about from one public work to another – apparently belonging to no country and having no home. He usually wore a white felt hat, the brim turned up all round – a headdress since become fashionable – a velveteen or jean square-tailed coat, a scarlet plush waistcoat with little black spots, and a bright-coloured handkerchief round his Herculean neck, when, as often happened, it was not left entirely bare. His corduroy breeches were retained in position by a leathern strap round the waist, and tied and buttoned at the knee, displaying beneath a solid calf and foot firmly encased in strong high-laced boots. Joining together in a 'butty gang,' some ten or twelve of these men would take a contract to cut out and remove so much 'dirt' – so they denominated earth-cutting – fixing their price according to the character of the 'stuff,' and the distance to which it had to be wheeled and tipped. The contract taken, every man put himself to his mettle; if any was found skulking, or not putting forth his full working power, he was ejected from the gang. Their powers of endurance were extraordinary. In times of emergency they would work for twelve and even sixteen hours, with only short intervals for meals; and the quantity of flesh-meat which they consumed was something enormous; but it was to their bones and muscles what coke is to the locomotive – the means of keeping up the steam.[5]

This is a very different picture from any we have had before and Smiles had ample opportunity to see the men at work. At the height of the construction period there were over 7,000 men working on the Leeds & Thirsk, many of them employed on the great Bramhope Tunnel. Smiles saw them as hard-working men doing a good job. Others visiting the same line at the same time came away with quite different impressions. A missionary who arrived at the diggings in November 1847 seems to have made his mind up before he even began to write his report:

> The Character of Navvies is so well known, that I need scarcely State, that Swearing, gambling, drunkenness & Sabbath breaking, prevail to a great extent among them. And it would have give me great pleasure to be able to state, that the last mentioned wicked practice was not observable upon the works … It is also well known that Ale, porter &c are sold in very many of the Huts on the Line.

It was certainly true that Sabbath breaking was not unknown. In 1839 four navvies who had been discovered working at Tiverton were brought before the magistrates by the resoundingly named 'Bath Association for the due observance of the Lord's day'. They were each fined 5s.[6] Interestingly, the railway companies themselves didn't actually forbid Sunday working. A contract between Benjamin Lawton and John Rush for work on the Newcastle & Berwick Railway is a very official document, written on expensive parchment, giving it an aura of great authority. It specifically states that Sunday working could be allowed with the company's permission. It seems that Sabbath breaking was not limited to the navvies themselves, and one cannot help wondering who told the Tiverton men to work that Sunday. This incident involved just four men, and reports of Sabbath breaking are rare. A very different story of how navvies spent their Sundays was told that same year and involved far greater numbers of men:

> On Sunday last the Rev. F. Close preached in a neat wooden temple near the Birmingham depot at the extreme end of the Queen's Road, Cheltenham, adjoining the Gloucester road; the object of which was to induce the men employed on these railway lines to attend and hear the word of God on Sunday afternoons. On this occasion several hundred persons were present chiefly of the class for the benefit of which the building was designed … The rev. gentleman

in conclusion stated that it was his intention to preach every Sunday afternoon in this little building now dedicated to God and he devoutly hoped some good would result from the service. Mr. Oldham, the contractor, then stated that as the building did not seem large enough he would be most happy to make it double the size by the following Sunday. We need not add that the offer was most readily accepted.[7]

Church services were also held for navvies at Bristol and Batheaston on the Great Western Railway, which were reported as being attended by hundreds of men. Perhaps not all navvies were as far beyond redemption as some reverend gentlemen seemed to believe.

Most commentators made no attempt to consider navvies as individuals, or even to distinguish between the different types of work that they did. To them anyone working on a railway who wasn't in charge of others was a navvy. In fact, as on the canals, the workforce was quite varied and different rates were paid for different jobs. The following rates were fairly typical of day rates in the early years:

Carpenters and smiths	3s 2d – 3s 6d
Strikers	2s
Navvies	2s – 2s 8d
Ganger	3s 6d
Horse keeper	2s 8d
Sawyer	3s – 3s 6d
Labourer	2s 6d [8]

Most of the categories are self-explanatory, but it is interesting to note that a navvy was not the same as an ordinary labourer. Those who railed against the navvies were certainly not making the same distinction. So it is not unreasonable to ask what was the main work that separated the navvy from everyone else who worked on the canals.

One of the main tasks that only the strongest could manage was filling wagons with spoil. It was here that experience and strength showed. On the Chester and Holyhead line, some of the work fell to experienced English navvies who had come from other workings, the rest to men recruited locally. When work started it needed five Welsh to fill a truck but only three English. Stephen Ballard, who was the principal assistant to Thomas Brassey, one of the greatest of all railway contractors, gave specific figures of what a team of experienced men could do:

Mr. Ballard's evidence with respect to the amount of labour done by the English navvies is very precise, and very valuable. He states as his opinion, that 'the labour which a navvy performs exceeds in severity almost any other description of work.' He says that 'a full day's work consists of fourteen sets a day. A 'set' is a number of wagons – in fact, a train. There are two men to a wagon. If the wagon goes out fourteen times, each man has to fill seven wagons in the course of the day. Each wagon contains two and a quarter cubic yards. The result is, that each man has to lift nearly twenty tons weight of earth on a shovel over his head into a wagon. The height of the lifting is about six feet. This is taking it at fourteen sets a day; but the navvies sometimes contrive to get through sixteen sets and there are some men who will accomplish that astonishing quantity of work by three or four o'clock in the afternoon – a result I believe, which is not nearly equalled by the workmen of any other country in the world.[9]

This is the kind of prodigious feat that set the railway navvy apart and gave him his unique identity. It is impossible to generalise on the subject of where navvies came from. The Irish, for example, were very strongly represented on lines in the north of England and in Scotland, but much less so in the south. On the Hawick line in Scotland there were 1,370 Scots at work, 731 Irish and only nine English. In the south-west of England well over a third of the navvies originally came from within 10 miles of where they were working. Some men may perhaps have signed up to work locally and, when the line was complete, went back to their old way of life. Others stayed navvies throughout their working lives. Richard Pearce, who gave evidence to the Parliamentary Committee looking into railway work, had begun on the Lancaster Canal at the age of twenty and thirty-two years later was still a navvy. Thomas Easton, who had been navvying for twenty-seven years, was asked if he had had many ups and downs. He replied: 'Yes, many up; not very far up; but many down.' Whatever he may have been responsible for after the day's work was done, and no one could pretend that the navvy was an ideal citizen, he certainly earned his title of King of the Labourers.

CHAPTER SIX

CONTRACTORS, GANGERS AND MEN

There was a hierarchy in railway works that had a direct effect on everything connected with the navvy life. The navvy was not touched very closely by the company men and may never have even seen the chief engineer. At the top of his particular pyramid was the main contractor, under him the subcontractors and below that the gangers with the men themselves at the base. Contractors came in many different guises. Some were in charge of great concerns, men whose names have come down to us as the giants of the railway world, notably Thomas Brassey and Samuel Morton Peto. Others have long been forgotten, their names occasionally appearing in company documents, usually when things went wrong. Some were born to comparatively wealthy families; others made their way up the hierarchical pyramid a step at a time. Some had resources that enabled them to cope with temporary financial problems; others succumbed the moment things went wrong. Which of the two latter classes a particular contractor fitted into made a huge difference to the navvy: with the first he would get his pay, with the latter he could be left with empty pockets.

The backgrounds of these two great contractors, Brassey and Peto — and their ultimate fortunes — were very different. Brassey came from a relatively wealthy landowning family in Cheshire. He left school at sixteen, was articled to a surveyor and land agent and eventually became a partner. His first encounter with a major civil engineering project came when he assisted in the surveying of the Holyhead Road, for which Telford was the chief engineer. But it was another famous engineer who set him on the path towards the career that was to make his fortune. Among the interests he looked after as a land agent was a stone quarry that attracted the attention of George Stephenson, who was looking for material for the Sankey viaduct on the Liverpool & Manchester Railway. It was Stephenson who suggested that he might apply for a railway contract and by 1834, when he was still only twenty-nine years old, he gained an important contract to build the Penkridge viaduct between Stafford and Wolverhampton, together with 10 miles of track. His professional contacts and family background meant that he had little trouble persuading a bank in Chester to provide the necessary capital for purchasing equipment. He was to remain a railway contractor for the rest of his working life and when he died in 1870 he left a fortune of over £3 million – well over £1 billion at today's prices.

Peto's background was much more humble. He attended the village school and had only two years of secondary education before being apprenticed to his uncle, a public works contractor. The business grew, and when the uncle died it passed to Peto and his cousin. Under their management it became ever more prosperous and among the prestigious works they took on was the construction of Nelson's monument in Trafalgar Square. Peto saw that there were great opportunities in railway construction, and he had an ulterior motive. He harboured political ambitions, and as a public works contractor and therefore employed by the government he was unable to stand for Parliament. But his cousin was less enthusiastic about railway building and the partnership was dissolved. Peto soon had a new partner, his brother-in-law Edward Betts. They began working railway contracts together in 1847.

Peto had a reputation for taking what were known as 'contractors' lines' – routes that were not necessarily attracting enthusiastic investors, but which provided work for him and his men. On these lines it was common practice to take a great deal of the fees in shares instead of cash. Ultimately this was his undoing. He took a contract for almost £6 million for the London, Chatham and Dover line, which lacked adequate real finance. After a period involving dubious manipulation of shares the company went bankrupt, taking Peto with it. He had achieved his political ambition, having been elected MP for Norwich, but now as a bankrupt he had to give up his seat. In his heyday he had been almost as powerful as Brassey, and the two had gone into partnership in constructing railways all over Europe. They had something else in common: both were famous for treating their staff fairly and generously, for which they earned the respect and loyalty of the men.

Men such as Brassey inevitably employed many subcontractors and he was conscious that these small concerns existed on a very narrow path between profit and loss. He could not personally supervise every contract and relied on his agents, but they were not empowered to alter any financial agreements that Brassey had made. Bargaining for a contract was a matter of luck as well as skill. What seemed like a good price because the work looked straightforward could turn out very differently if unexpectedly difficult ground

In the 1840s Peto held thirty-five railway contracts worth approximately £20 million.

was met. One of Brassey's subcontractors found himself in just that situation, where instead of just light soil that had to be removed he found himself faced with heavy clay and rock. He carried on with the work anyway, without complaint, certain that when Brassey did appear on site he would be dealt with fairly:

> He came, walking along the line as usual, with a number of followers, and on coming to the cutting he looked round, counted the number of wagons at the work, scanned the cutting, and took stock of the nature of the stuff. 'This is very hard,' said he to the sub-contractor. 'Yes, it is a pretty deal harder than I bargained for.' Mr. Brassey would linger behind allowing the others to go on, and then commenced the following conversation. 'What is your price for this cutting?' 'So much a yard, sir.' 'It is very evident that you are not getting it out for that price. Have you asked for any advance to be made to you for this rock?' 'Yes, sir, but I can make no sense of them.' 'If you say that your price is so much, it is quite clear that you do not do it for that. I am glad that you have persevered with it, but I shall not alter your price; it must remain as it is, but the rock must be measured for you twice; will that do for you?' 'Yes, very well indeed, and I am very much obliged to you, sir.' 'Very well; go on; you have done well in persevering, and I shall look to you again'.[1]

It was said that these agreements sometimes cost Brassey as much as £1,000, and being himself on a fixed-price contract he had no means of reclaiming it from the company. The subcontractor got paid double for the rock he had to remove, and by showing loyalty to Brassey was rewarded with the promise of more work later. Brassey, although it cost him a great deal in terms of cash, got work that was well and thoroughly done. He also ensured that he had the respect of everyone who worked for him: 'as he went along the line in these inspections, he remembered even the navvies, and saluted them by their names.' The value of subcontracts varied between £5,000 and £25,000 and each subcontractor employed between 100 and 300 men, though the former was more common. On some lines, division went even further, with subcontractors letting out work to sub-subcontractors, though this was a practice of which Brassey disapproved very strongly, and the subcontractor who wanted to work for him again was well advised to take notice. Brassey chose his men carefully and only handed out work that he was sure was well within the capability of the subcontractor to perform, without having to let out any of the work to others.

Peto, like Brassey, took an active interest in the welfare of the navvies who worked for him:

> Mr. Peto has been a positive benefactor to the railway labourer. Believing that the 14,000 navigators – the average number he employed for several years – had

minds as well as bodies, he acted up to that creed. He supplied them with books, and engaged for them teachers. He formed sick-clubs, introduced benefit-societies, and taught them the use of savings-banks. He built temporary cottages, and let them at proper prices. He took care that the apartments should be tenanted with due regard to decency; and the consequence was, in the words of Bishop Stanley, 'the gin shops were deserted and schools were full'.[2]

He encouraged men to better themselves, and some did, though whether with the success that this rose-coloured account suggests is perhaps a little dubious: 'some of the most beautiful country seats in England belong to men who trundled their barrow, who delved with the spade and pick-axe, and blasted the rock.' Some of the contractors who gave evidence to the Parliamentary Committee of 1846 looking into the conditions of railway navvies found that some contractors had indeed come up the hard way.[3] John Sharp had come from Durham to take a job on the Great Western Railway at Keynsham. He was an experienced navvy and was soon made foreman, but in his own words 'saw clearly that things were going wrong'. He decided he could do better than the man he was working for and managed to get a subcontract at the works.

There was another aspect of the relationship between contractor and men that distinguished both Brassey and Peto from others: they insisted on paying wages weekly and in cash. Peto arranged to have his payments made every Saturday afternoon, and this required a system that was kept under strict control. He had an agent who was placed in charge of the whole project, and sub-agents under him who were each responsible for between 8 and 9 miles of line; timekeepers were employed at 2-mile intervals to record the amount of work done. Each week the sub-agents made up the weekly pay packets and handed them to the gangers. Peto made sure that the navvies got their fair wage and that there was a small profit for the gangers. The timekeepers were on hand to ensure the gangers didn't take a bigger slice than they were entitled to. It was a system that was accepted as fair by all concerned and worked in everyone's interests.

Many contractors paid far less regularly, perhaps only once a month or so. The result was that the men who had been short of cash suddenly had quite a lot of it. They were not thrifty savers by nature, so they were inclined to go out drinking and stay out while the money lasted. Peto, by paying regularly, was able to insist on the navvies keeping their side of the bargain, by turning up ready for work on the Monday morning. Anyone who failed to appear, unless he had very good reason, was promptly sent packing. Peto was also aware that the men were easily cheated out of their money, so he did his best to ensure that they were well supplied at reasonable prices. He sent his agents to the nearest town to say: 'at such a place or such a place I shall be paying away 500l. or 600l. a week to the men, and it will be in your interest to take care the men are well supplied ... At one place, I saw several butchers' men crying out "Who wants a fine leg of mutton?"[4]

Many other contractors neither paid regularly nor in coin of the realm, and this was to be a source of friction that could even lead to rioting. With few resources, the smaller contractors relied on the company measuring the work and paying up promptly so that they had enough cash to pay the navvies. When that didn't happen, there was a serious problem: 'Everyone that wants some thing of me is looking for it this pay which i will not be able to pay unless you Dow somethink for me.'[5] Some companies always tried to let contracts to the big contractors; others were content to parcel everything out in small lots, but this could create problems when the small contractors lacked the necessary resources. This was what happened on the line from London to Southampton:

> While the work was easy, while prices and pay remained depressed, while nothing extraordinary occurred the work was done; but when any engineering novelty arose, the poor contractor was powerless. The smallest difficulty stayed him; the slightest danger paralysed him. He could not complete his contract; he lacked resources to pay the penalty; the works were often stopped; the directors as often in despair.[6]

In these circumstances it was not only the directors who were in despair. If a contractor went bust then the first to suffer were the gangs who didn't get paid. Even a temporary shortage of funds could cause major problems. One small contractor tried to do his best when he was short of cash by paying the men half their wages and promising more shortly. Not surprisingly, the men were unimpressed:

> The men is coming on me for all there [sic] wages and as there is a parte cash in hand for work done since it was measured to be payed on Saturday first i hope that you will take it in consideration so that the men may get there wages for they threaten to Distress me to the Justice meeting i was told to pay half of the wages and i have and they are not content.[7]

The man was doing his best, but had found himself in the position in which many of his fellows found themselves – of simply not having the cash available. Sometimes the subcontractor had fallen behind the schedule set for him, so the main contractor hadn't come through with the funds. In other cases, the main contractor had simply delayed making the payments for no particular reason, apart from the very common desire to keep their money in their own coffers for as long as possible. The small men simply didn't have the capital to see them through such difficulties. When the big men didn't pay the little men, the workers at the end of the pay chain suffered. There were also some subcontractors who were simply downright dishonest and did a runner. John

Sharp, mentioned above, gave evidence about 'Ready-money Tom' who lived up to his nickname by disappearing, taking £150 with him and leaving his men unpaid. Another contractor rented horses from local farms, but when he left the diggings the horses went with him. According to one of the missionaries who came to preach to the navvies, it was not unknown for subcontractors to take £1,000 or more and buy themselves a ticket to America and a new life out of the reach of the law. Needless to say, the navvies were well aware of the situation and kept their eyes open for likely defectors.

Benley and Leech were just two such subcontractors, working on the East Lancashire Railway at Hepton in 1846. Rumours spread among the navvies that they were planning to abscond. When pay day arrived at The Angel inn, where the two men were staying, a few wages were paid and then nothing more. Suspicions were confirmed when it was discovered that the two had been sneaking their furniture and belongings out of the inn on the previous night. The navvies were not going to let them get away. They were taken into the billiard room at the inn and a guard was set, who decided to make a bit of money on the side by charging a halfpenny for anyone who wanted to come and see the prisoners for themselves. Over 400 navvies came to enjoy the misery of their would-be swindlers, netting the guards a useful 17s profit. By Sunday night, the local magistrates decided that things had gone far enough and persuaded the navvies to deliver their two prisoners to the police station, on the undertaking that they would appear before the bench the next day.

The navvies filled every corner of the court, hoping to see justice done. What emerged was a familiar story. The subcontractors had fallen behind with the work, the contractors had not paid up and there was no cash in the coffers. To the magistrates the matter was simple: no offence had been committed, so it was a matter for the civil courts to deal with. Leech and Benley were taken back to the police station, not to be charged but simply for their own safety. Leech was presumably unconvinced that the police could do much if the navvies got really worked up, so he hopped through a window and legged it as fast as he could go, but not fast enough. The navvies caught up with him and took him back to his former 'prison' at The Angel. Once again the police had to come in and rescue him. The situation as far as the navvies were concerned was hopeless. It was all very well the magistrates recommending the civil court, but they had no money to pay lawyers and had the

The 2-mile-long Bramhope Tunnel was an immense undertaking of which the Leeds & Thirsk company must have been proud, for its northern portal was given an elaborate Gothic treatment with towers and battlements. A miniature version of it can be seen in nearby Otley churchyard as a memorial to the twenty-three men who died during construction.

more urgent matter of not even having cash to buy food. They had done work, ultimately, for the main contractor, so they applied to him for help. He ignored the moral argument and fell back on the legal position that he had not employed them himself so he owed them nothing. The navvies understood enough of the law to know that this was an argument they could not win. On the rare occasions when contractors and subcontractors were taken to court for non-payment, the men might win the case but still come away empty-handed. There were several cases where this happened and the contractors simply told the magistrates that they had no jurisdiction over them and refused to pay, and that was the end of the matter. In any case, there was little point in the navvies pursuing the two subcontractors since the pair had no money anyway. The best they could do was to pack up their things and look for work somewhere else down the line. Contracting and subcontracting was a system for organising labour that suited many, from the company down, but when things went wrong it was always the men at the end of the payment chain who suffered most.

Even at the lowest level, things could go badly wrong. Brassey may have taken steps to ensure that the gangers dealt fairly with the men under them, but many contractors took no interest. In his evidence to the 1846 Committee, the Revd Robert Wilson described pay day on the Swaffham and Dereham line, where the men were paid in a crowded room. The money was thrust into their hands and they were hustled away before they had a chance to count it. One navvy was owed £2 9s, but when he came to count it he was £1 short. The ganger disputed his claim, and of course the navvy had no means of proving his point. This appears to be an exception. In general, gangers acted fairly, and if there was an argument it was settled, as one navvy put it, by a bang on the head and a few pints afterwards.

The railway construction world sometimes appears to have been permanently beset by squabbles, arguments and major disagreements, usually involving those higher up the ladder complaining about what was happening on the rung below. The navvy was in the unfortunate position of being on the bottom rung, with no one lower down to blame when things went wrong. The chief engineer generally tried to distance himself from the day-to-day management of the men on the ground. He had more important things to deal with as a rule than arbitrating between his own assistants and the various contractors. When a resident engineer complained about Hemming, a contractor on the Cheltenham & Gloucester Railway, and appealed to his superior Isambard Kingdom Brunel for help, he got a stern lecture. Brunel pointed out that, while he was happy to arbitrate where contracts and disputes about measurements of the work performed were concerned, he was not prepared to get involved over differences of opinion which lacked hard evidence. He then proceeded to lay down exactly how the sensible engineer should deal with a contractor:

You must be quite aware that unless a contractor is managed with great care and unless he feels confidence in those placed over him by the Comp[y] the works cannot proceed satisfactorily. When a man like Hemming of no great strength of will and from ill health not over strong in mind or body has in his hands such an important part of the whole line and where the progress of the works depend entirely upon him accordingly the interests of the company require that he should be handled with the utmost tenderness. His losses become the Company's in fact through him and if he is harassed by orders difficult to obey or inconvenienced by the want of money or dispirited by harsh treatment or by what he only fancies harshness work suffers and thereby the Company suffers. Now, Hemming, is peculiarly a case in point. We know that he has not a large capital that if he loses much it will be beyond his means and upon the comp[y] will once paid fall the consequences. If he loses time we are the sufferers, he cannot compensate us. If he should be entirely stopped the loss to the Com[y] in money would be increases in time irretrievable. He is the horse we have in harness and upon which we must depend and therefore whatever may be his weak points or his vices or whatever our right to treat him as we choose it is our interest not to overdrive him or to starve him, to be contented with his utmost altho' this may fall far short of what we originally calculated upon.[8]

These are the words of an eminently reasonable man putting forward a practical way of dealing with the many disagreements that inevitably arose between the engineering staff and the contractors. If such advice had been regularly followed throughout the system, then disputes could have been kept to a minimum and those that did emerge could have been settled amicably. Not every engineer followed this sensible advice and one man who flagrantly ignored it was the man himself, I.K. Brunel.

The following story involves the construction of the Oxford, Worcester & Wolverhampton Railway (OW & WR), one of the further-flung outposts of the Great Western empire. It was a line on which few things went right, and when it was eventually completed it was well over budget. The biggest problem centred on the Mickleton Tunnel between Evesham and Chipping Campden.[9] Things started badly and got worse.

The first contractors lasted just four months before running out of money. The contract was taken over by a consortium of William Williams, Simon Aykroyd and David Price. The omens were not good. It soon became clear that they too were under-funded. The whole contract for over £100,000 was handed to them in February 1847, but they had to rely on a firm of solicitors in Wigan for backing and even then had to borrow £9,000 from the OW & WR just to pay for the equipment abandoned by the first contractors. Not surprisingly, things did not go well, largely because the contractors completely failed to organise the workforce in an efficient manner, neglecting even to appoint a foreman to take control. As a result, the reports from the workings

1 Men at work in the Islington Tunnel on the Regent's Canal, which was completed in 1820. (British Waterways)

2 Repairing a lock on the Grand Union Canal, under the gaze of several small boys. (British Waterways)

3 Constructing the canal basin on the Rochester Canal in Manchester. (British Waterways)

4 Navvies on the Manchester Ship Canal. (British Waterways)

5 Barrow runs on the London & Birmingham Railway. (National Railway Museum, York)

6 Navvies at work in a deep cutting in Camden Town, London & Birmingham Railway. (National Railway Museum, York)

7 Tipping soil at an embankment, Great Central Railway. (Leicestershire Record Office)

8 'Cut and fill' on the Great Central Railway: the photograph clearly shows how the spoil from the cutting has been used for the next embankment. (Leicestershire Record Office)

9 Floating the massive tube for Robert Stephenson's bridge at Conwy; a similar technique was used for the bigger Menai Straits Bridge. (Elton Collection, Ironbridge Gorge Museum)

10 The rescue party approaching the trapped workers in the Severn Tunnel. (Anthony Burton)

11 A navvy wife outside one of the temporary cabins on the Great Central Railway. (Leicestershire Record Office)

12 A Navvy Mission hall on the Great Central Railway. (Leicestershire Record Office)

13 An enterprising liquor seller on the Manchester Ship Canal. (Manchester Ship Canal Co.)

14 A contractor's train crosses a trestle viaduct on the Union Pacific Railway. (Union Pacific Historical Collection)

15 Filling spoil wagons on the Manchester Ship Canal. (Manchester Ship Canal Co.)

16 Mechanisation on the Manchester Ship Canal: machinery would soon be bringing the old navvy way of life to an end. (Manchester Ship Canal Co.)

spoke of the 'apathetic spirit' of the men. Brunel railed against their misman-
agement, pointing out that it was in their interest to get a grip on things or
else the contractors faced ruin. The engineers had done their best to encourage them, but instead of improving, things only seemed to get steadily worse.
In 1849 Aykroyd and Price quit and Williams formed a new partnership with
Robert Marchant. Brunel must have been hopeful that this would be a turn
for the better, for Marchant was actually employed as an engineering assistant
on the line, had been highly critical of how things had been managed in the
past – and was even a distant relation of the Brunel family. But fresh troubles
appeared that were no fault of the new contractors: the company ran out of
cash and the works came to a standstill.

Williams and Marchant agreed to carry out maintenance work for the time
being, but started a legal action for compensation for the stoppage. When
work restarted things progressed no faster under the new contractors than
they had under the old, to Brunel's increasing annoyance. In July 1851 Brunel
issued an ultimatum: put more men to work to get the job finished, or abandon the contract. The contractors did neither. The situation then deteriorated
very dramatically. Marchant's agent complained to the Chipping Campden
magistrates that Brunel had sent a new subcontractor into the tunnel who
was threatening to take over the whole of the works by force. The authorities
took the threat seriously and they were right to do so. Brunel was advancing at the head of an army of some 200 navvies, armed with cudgels and
encouraged by liberal doses of free beer. Brunel agreed to negotiate, but there
was little sign of any agreement being reached when the magistrates themselves arrived, accompanied by special constables armed with cutlasses. They
read the Riot Act and the two sides separated. It was only a temporary truce:
more navvies poured into the district and Marchant found himself with about
150 men against Brunel with 2,000. Brunel probably had very little faith in
the law acting even-handedly since at least one of the special constables was
R.M. Marchant, a close relation of the opposition. Nevertheless, there is no
doubt that in being prepared to use force to grab back the contract Brunel
was acting illegally. There are varying reports of what happened in the first few
hours. One local paper spoke of small skirmishes, but *The Times* reported that
one navvy's head was 'nearly severed in two', limbs broken and 'great cruelty
at times perpetrated'.

There was only ever going to be one outcome. Marchant withdrew his men
and agreed to leave the matter of compensation to arbitrators. The tunnel contract went to the well-established and reliable partnership of Peto and Betts,
who took on most of the old workforce, thus avoiding any more trouble.
Arbitration duly took place. Many commentators felt that Marchant had some
rights on his side; even if he had been incompetent that did not justify Brunel
using brute force to settle matters. But Marchant lost, and the result was his
financial ruin. The OW & WR gave Brunel a bonus for his part in the fracas.

One suspects that the engineer rather enjoyed the whole episode and relished his role as temporary general of a navvy army.

Brunel was not the first to use navvies in this way. It was not uncommon during the planning stage of any railway to find landowners doing their best to keep the surveyors at bay. George Stephenson had found that one noble lord had ordered his gamekeepers to fire guns at random through the night to stop anyone sneaking in under darkness. The Duke of Cleveland took an equally firm line for his estates near Barnard Castle, ordering his staff to use any means to keep the surveyors out. He was aggrieved to find the company resorting to subterfuge: 'You have attempted to make a survey near my property by stealth, and to make the fraud more complete you ordered your surveyor to put on the dress of one of the Gaffers and Miners, pretending that he was taking a Government survey.'[10] The idea of railway surveyors scurrying around in disguise is quite comical, but there was nothing in the least amusing about the events that occurred during a Midland Railway survey in 1845.

The company wanted to take the line from Peterborough to Leicester through land at Stapleton Park owned by Lord Harborough. His Lordship had just spent a lot of money on improving the park and the last thing he wanted was to see a railway coming anywhere near it, and did all he could to prevent the survey going ahead. One transport system already went through the area, the Oakham Canal, and the company had the bright idea of sending their surveyors along the towpath to carry out the work. They were stopped by Lord Harborough's men who claimed ownership of that as well. This was a blatant lie: the land was owned by the canal company. There was a confrontation, during which one of the railway men drew a pistol, but the estate workers stood firm deciding, quite reasonably, that no one was going to risk a murder charge just to carry out a survey. The unfortunate pistol-toting surveyor did, however, end up spending the weekend in gaol.

The company decided there was now no option. If they wanted to carry out a survey then they had to use force. They gathered together a band of navvies and marched to Saxby Bridge, and at the same time a rival army of estate workers marched forward to confront them. As at Mickleton, the local police were able to get between the two sides and nothing worse than a few scuffles occurred before the two sides withdrew. But that was not the end of the affair. The company decided that they could win the day if they made a fresh attempt to get on the land by sneaking up at dawn. The estate workers were ready for them, and the only people who were caught by surprise were the police. There was a battle, in which the two sides attacked each other with anything from pickaxe handles to fence posts. In the confusion, the surveyors managed somehow to get their work done. It was a pyrrhic victory. Six navvies were sent to prison and in the end the line did not encroach on the parkland, but swept round it in an extravagant bend, which became known as Lord Harborough's Curve.

Both these instances show that whatever condemnations society might heap on riotous navvies, perfectly respectable gentlemen were prepared to make use of their muscle power when it suited their interests. These gentlemen might also cynically have thought that if there was going to be trouble with the law, it would be the navvies on the ground not the men who had instructed them who would end up behind bars. The navvies were, however, just as capable of starting battles on their own account, particularly where money was concerned. Everyone in the construction chain wanted to make as much money from their particular link as they possibly could. It started with the company, who put the work out to tender and generally accepted the lowest offer. The would-be contractors had to make a fine judgement: put a high price forward and you could make a good profit, but it risked not getting the contract; put too low a price forward and you could finish up out of pocket. It was not an exact science. One successful contractor, Joseph Firbanks, told the story of how a Mr Wythes worked out his bid.[11] He started out thinking that he could do the work for £18,000, but his wife said she thought that was too low, so they settled on £20,000. He thought the whole thing over, considered what things might go wrong along the way and decided that perhaps it would be safer to make it £40,000. He and his wife then went off to bed intending to make a final decision in the morning. After a good night's sleep they decided that they might just as well double up again and duly put in a bid at £80,000. They got the contract. Presumably Mr Wythes made a good profit and would not have been too anxious about the rates he might have to pay any subcontractors. Others did not allow such extravagant margins so had to be a good deal more cautious. They had to strike the best bargains they could with the subcontractors, and they in their turn had to begin negotiations with the gangers in order to get men at the lowest possible wages. That was when the trouble started. It could be no more than a fistfight between a few men, but it could be a good deal more serious, as happened on the Great Western Railway in 1838:

On Monday last a number of navigators working on the Great Western Railway, amounting to upwards of 300, principally natives of the County of Gloucester, tumultuously assembled, and made an attack on the workmen employed at Tunnel no. 3 Keynsham, who are most of them from Devonshire, and the lower parts of Somerset. The ostensible motive for the attack was a belief that the latter were working under price; to this was added a local or county feud, as the rallying cry of onslaught was 'Gloucester against Devon'. The result was a regular fight with various dangerous weapons, ready at hand, such as spades, pickaxes, crowbars, &c – The contest was long and severe, in which several were most dangerously hurt, & one man was obliged to be taken to the Infirmary, but no one was killed. The insubordination continued for several succeeding days, and was not repressed without the aid of the military.[12]

It turned out that the work had been allocated to gangers who were to be paid a fixed price per yard, but the Devon men had been using a type of heavy drill, known as a jumper, which was common in the copper mines of their home county. As a result, they were working faster than the Gloucester men and so earning more money. The result of this fracas was that one man suffered a serious spinal injury. The same report went on to list even worse trouble at the other end of the line:

> It would seem by the fact of a similar riot having taken place at the same time on the London end of the line, that there was some secret understanding and concert among the discontented workmen. The following is from a London Paper: – 'We regret to state that a most desperate and alarming affray took place on the evening of Sunday last, betwixt the English and Irish labourers employed upon the GWR. It was again renewed on Monday and many of the results are anticipated to be fatal. The riot is understood to have arisen in consequence of the Irish party having proposed to work for lower wages than their English fellow-labourers. The atrocities upon both sides have been of the most brutal and unmanly description, and but for the interference of the local authorities aided by a squadron of the 12th Lancers, the most lamentable consequences must have ensued. Twenty-four of the rioters have been committed to Clerkenwell Prison, where they will now remain until a further examination.'

The uneasy relationship that could exist between employers and men and between men and their fellow navvies could lead to the sort of dramatic events that were reported in the press. But sensational events were not the norm for navvy life; most of the time work simply carried on, moving the tracks across more and more of the British countryside. It is time to turn away from conflict and look at the everyday working life of the navvies.

CHAPTER SEVEN

WORKING ON THE LINE

In some respects railway construction was very similar to canal construction. Engineers needed to keep their routes on the level as far as possible and often the railway men simply followed the paths set out by their predecessors on the canals. When Robert Stephenson began to plan his line from Birmingham to London he closely followed that of the Grand Junction Canal laid out by William Jessop half a century earlier. He faced precisely the same obstacles, but the scale of works had changed dramatically. For example, Jessop had tackled the passage through the Chiltern Hills by means of a deep cutting at Tring. He had made his task a bit easier by a gentle climb up the slope through locks to the south of the cutting and had emerged at the northern end to another flight of locks that took the canal steeply downhill into the next valley. Railway locomotives cannot climb up and down hills in the same way, and the days when stationary engines might be used to help with haulage were over. So Stephenson had to start his cutting at a lower level to make his way through the ridge. Not only did it have to be longer and deeper than the canal cutting, it had to be wider as well to take the double tracks. It was estimated that 1.4 million cubic yards of chalk were removed. Walk down the road from Tring station to the canal and you can still make a direct comparison between the two routes. The same increase in scale applied to all the other major features along the way: banks were higher, viaducts taller and longer than the equivalent aqueducts, and tunnels had to be bigger to accommodate locomotives and carriages instead of low-decked boats. It all added up to moving a lot more earth and creating far more imposing structures.

Canals crossed rivers on aqueducts and the mightiest of them all was Pontcysyllte that carried the Ellesmere canal across the Dee valley near Llangollen. At just over 1,000ft long and rising to a maximum height of 120ft it was one of the wonders of the age. The actual water is held in an iron trough carried on nineteen stone arches. Telford, the engineer mainly responsible for the design, economised on material by making the trough just wide enough to take one boat at a time. This was not a problem in practice: boats could wait at one end until the passage was clear and then move into the trough. Systems such as this were obviously not practical on the main-line railways, so the equivalent viaducts had to be built to take double tracks. The Digswell viaduct near Welwyn in Hertfordshire dwarfs Pontcysyllte but does not look as dramatic as the famous aqueduct. The grandeur of the work really becomes clear, however, when you look at the statistics. Designed by William Cubitt and built by Brassey and his men, it is 100ft high, 4,560ft long and carried on forty brick arches comprising an amazing 13 million bricks. In canal construction days the bricks would all have been made on site. The clay would have been dug up by navvies, pounded to create a uniform consistency to get rid of any air bubbles and then each brick would have been made by hand in moulds. They were then left to dry out before being fired in situ in 'clamps' – simple vertical kilns with a coal fire at the bottom and the 'green' bricks stacked above, the whole thing being closed off by burned bricks. The whole process lasted for days, and the results were very uneven, which is why when we see an old canal bridge today, the bricks with which it was built can range in colour from a bright orange to a dark red. Fortunately for the railway builders, advances in brick-making made their work more efficient and produced more consistent results.

In the early nineteenth century new inventions mechanised many of the processes. The clay was mixed in steam-powered pug mills and then fed into extrusion machines. There the clay was forced through a die from which it emerged as a long rectangular block that was then cut by wires to make individual bricks. Firing was now carried out in greatly improved kilns, ensuring a far greater uniformity. We actually know a great deal about brick production in Britain in the early nineteenth century thanks to the statistics for the brick tax. In 1821 records show that just over 913 million bricks were taxed: by 1840 that number had almost doubled, and most of the increase was down to railway construction.

Mechanisation and specialist manufacturers saved the navvies a great deal of hard labour, though there was still the job of carting the bricks to the site, unloading them and getting them to the bricklayers. The hard work of the navvy has been a theme running through this book, but it is worth putting in perspective. The bricks that were sent to the construction site were not produced without a great deal of suffering. In 1871 the great philanthropist Lord Shaftesbury put forward a motion in the House of Lords to ban the use of child labour in the industry. He described the scene that had horrified him into taking up the cause:

> I went down to a brickfield and made a considerable inspection. I first saw, at a distance, what appeared to be eight or ten pillars of clay … On walking up, I found to my astonishment that these pillars were human beings. They were

so like the ground on which they stood, their features were so indistinguish-able, their dress so besoiled and covered with clay that, until I approached and saw them move, I believed them to be the products of the earth ... I saw little children, three-parts naked, tottering under the weight of wet clay, some of it on their heads, and some on their shoulders, and little girls with large masses of wet, cold, and dripping clay pressing on their abdomens.[1]

Lord Shaftesbury's campaign succeeded.

The great viaducts occupied a large workforce over long periods of time, and the consequences will be discussed later. These, however, only represent a fraction of the works being carried out up and down the different lines. It has been estimated that between 1840 and 1850 some 50,000 bridges were constructed, either to carry the rails over obstacles or to carry roads over the tracks. That is more bridges than had existed in Britain throughout history and each of those bridges used an average of 300,000 bricks. Even such star-tling figures seem insignificant compared with those for lining a tunnel, which worked out at roughly 14 million per mile.[2] It is difficult to imagine how this number of bricks could ever have been supplied using the methods of the canal age. While it made sense to bring in bricks from specialist brickworks for the viaducts, the same was not necessarily true when it came to creating tunnel linings, especially when a great deal of clay was already being excavated on site. Some engineers decided to set up their own brickworks, but using the new technology instead of the cruder system of the canal builders. When Robert Stephenson sent in his report on the work needed for Kilsby Tunnel on the London & Birmingham Railway in April 1836, he put forward the fol-lowing proposal:

To erect a steam clay mill with kilns etc sufficient to supply 30,000 bricks per diem; say total quantity of bricks required 20,000,000 then 10,000,000 to be made the first season, and supposing 6,000,000 may be obtained from the open cuttings at the end of the tunnel and the neighbouring brickworks, 4,000,000 will be required from tunnel clay, then average number of working days in the season, say 15 x 30,000 = 4,500,000.

The railway construction industry not only employed huge numbers, perhaps as many as a quarter of a million, but also provided work for all those who sup-plied the basic materials.

As the work demanded by railway construction closely mirrored that of canal construction, it is hardly surprising that the canal navvies adapted easily to work on the new transport system. The technology was mostly the same: only the scale differed. The one time the railway navvy had the advantage over his canal counterpart was when he came to level ground: he didn't have to dig a ditch. That does not mean that overall he had less hard labour to face.

There was one part of the construction process that was new: railway track had to be laid. The early technique of setting rails on stone blocks soon gave way to the more familiar transverse sleepers, with metal chairs to hold the rails in place. The exception was on the Great Western where Brunel, never a man to meekly follow others, devised his own system of longitudinal sleepers running the whole length of the line. Rails, too, changed over the years, but by the 1740s the bull-head rail introduced by Joseph Locke was proving the most popular. In cross section the first versions of the rail looked a bit like a dumbbell, the idea being that when one side was worn, the rail could be turned upside down. In practice this never worked, and in later designs the top was narrower than the bottom. There were many different versions, with weights ranging from 42 to 82lb per yard. Lengths also varied, but 60ft eventually became an accepted length. That means that a single rail could weigh as much as 1,640lb, which is roughly three-quarters of a ton. Track layers had to lay down the heavy wooden sleepers, place the chairs that held the rails in place – and they could weigh 50lb or more each – and then manhandle the heavy rails into place. The chairs then had to be spiked securely to the sleepers. For every mile of double track the navvies had to carry over 250 tons of rail. And laying the track was not the end of the process: it had to be ballasted. Crushed stone was laid all round the sleepers and under the rails. It served to help with drainage, stabilise the track when trains were passing and suppress weed. Quarry stone had to be broken into small pieces and laid to at least 6in thick. The navvies might not have had to dig out a canal, but there was no shortage of work requiring just as much brawn.

In the deep cuttings, the work was hard and dangerous. The job generally began by cutting a 'gullet', a narrow cutting just wide enough to take a single-track line for horses to haul away wagons full of spoil. The wagon train was controlled by a brakeman who perched on the last of the loaded trucks and used a long lever to apply a brake to the wheels. It sounds like the sort of job any navvy might volunteer for, when the alternative was shovelling spoil all day long, but it was not the easy option it might have seemed: 'His duty was … anything but pleasant for, what with the roughness of the roads, and the action of the springless vehicles on which he rides, the shaking he receives in his journey seems sufficient to reduce every joint in his body to a most unsatisfactory condition of laxity.'[3]

The village of Kilsby near Rugby was all but overwhelmed when over 1,000 men descended on it to work on a tunnel on the London & Birmingham Railway.

Blisworth cutting on the London & Birmingham Railway was described by one of the engineers, Robert Rawlinson, as involving 'considerable loss of life'.[4] The men worked their way down through gravel, clay and marl and eventually came to the limestone bedrock. Material was shifted using pickaxes and 100,000lb of gunpowder and the spoil removed up barrow runs. The most dangerous part of the work was attacking a vertical face of clay and chalk that could be as much as 12ft high. The technique was to carve down the vertical sides of the face, then cut channels at intervals along the bottom to undermine it. When the remaining pillars were knocked away, the whole face should collapse. The ideal scenario was for it to topple, coming away in a piece rather than simply subsiding. It made the work quicker, which meant that the navvies could earn more money on the contract. A man placed at the top of the face was there to give warning that the face was starting to move, theoretically providing enough time for the men at the bottom to get clear. If undermining failed to shift it, then it had to be levered away. But the whole process of bringing down a tall face was fraught with danger. If the men carried out too much undercutting before they were ready to knock out the supporting columns the face could collapse on top of them, which was why the same engineer reiterated that he had 'known many men killed, and others seriously lamed'. He also gave his opinion that where accidents did occur they were always the fault of the men involved, often because they were inexperienced. He did not, it seems, ask why inexperienced men were put in that situation in the first place. No one appears to have kept any accurate records of deaths and injuries. A surgeon who dealt with men injured on the Sheffield and Manchester line asked what happened when men lost limbs. He replied: 'the contractor would have made some inquiry, but I never heard of any.' As for the dead, as they didn't require his services he took no notice of them. He also ended his parliamentary evidence by saying that he thought accidents were always the men's own fault, probably brought about by drinking.[5] He was clearly not a man to turn to for sympathy.

The men who worked the deep cuttings were proud of their abilities and did not hesitate to make sure that anyone who joined the gang was as tough as they were. Rawlinson reported that few locals were tempted to take on the work, in spite of the high wages, and those who did were the 'worst characters'. They were given the simplest task of filling the barrows, but even then they had to prove their worth:

> There is a system called 'harrying' the men. If it is barrow work, for instance, they will so overload the barrow and overwork them, that if he is not accustomed to it he will sink under it … if he is not a man of extraordinary muscular energy, he cannot stand that system.[6]

The spoil from the cuttings was not simply material to be dumped anywhere convenient. Like the canals, railways made extensive use of 'cut and fill', so the material would be used to build up an embankment over the adjoining valley. Any turf removed in creating the cutting was carefully stored and kept ready to put in place on the sides of the newly constructed embankment, where the roots would help in the process of stabilisation and the plant cover would reduce the risk of erosion. The rest of the material would go to make up the bank itself. This was an occupation that carried its own hazards. One advantage of railway construction was that, as the line progressed and tracks were laid, locomotives could be brought in to help with tasks like moving the spoil. That did not necessarily make life easier for the men who had to hurl the material into the high-sided wagons, but it did speed things up a great deal. But once the locomotive was near the end of the bank under construction, the points were switched, allowing the wagons to be uncoupled and pulled the rest of the way by horses. Often the horses had to work up a gradient and, straining to haul the truck, they had to get up a good trot. It was the job of the person in charge to unhitch the horse at the last moment, pulling it to one side to allow the truck to carry on under its own momentum. The truck was specially designed so that when it hit an obstacle set at the end of the line, it tipped up, spewing its material down the bank. It was a matter of good judgement. Rawlinson in his evidence to Parliament described what could happen when things went wrong. Sometimes the person was too late unhitching the horse, and when that happened man, horse and wagon all went crashing down the slope. Often the job of looking after the horses went to boys, not men, and they faced other dangers as well:

> A very young man John Allen one of the drivers on that part of the Great Western Railway now constructing by the side of the canal on the road to Bathampton was on Thursday night brought to the Bath Hospital having met with a frightful accident. His foot slipped and he fell when a whole train of tram wagons went over his right arm and thigh completely smashing both limbs. The loss of blood was so great that he died soon after he reached the hospital.[7]

The 'spreaders' at the foot of the bank had to be equally alert. They wanted to get in quickly to deal with the spoil as it was tipped, but needed to get out of the way before the next truck arrived. Sometimes the men at the top decided to speed the whole process up, running up to ten trucks one after the other. They had a special name for that: 'We'll run 'em in a red 'un.' It does not take a great act of imagination to work out what that phrase might mean.

Accidents were not limited to the construction site. Where material wasn't available as spoil from the cuttings it had to be acquired from elsewhere – and the quickest method was to open up a quarry and blast it out. In August 1840 that was what was happening on the line from Exeter to Bristol, when unfortunately one of the men, John Carse, didn't get out of the way fast enough when the powder train was lit. According to the coroner's report, 'the poor fellow was blown upwards between 20 and 30 feet and killed on the spot'.

Not all engineers even approved of building high banks at all. Robert Stephenson, for one, preferred crossing valleys on bridges. He went to look at the Bishop Auckland & Weardale Railway and was dismayed to find banks as high as 60ft being constructed, where he would have recommended viaducts:

> The only case in which I can conceive the propriety of this principle to be questionable is when the material is sand or Gravel, easily obtained, and the base upon which the Embankments are to be formed undoubtedly sound – On the Auckland and Weardale Railway however these conditions are not only all wanting but in lieu of them they have slippery material easily affected by wet weather and obviously treacherous foundations.[8]

It was not all hard work from morning to night every day of the week down in the cuttings. An experienced contractor explained what could happen in bad weather:

> If we have a gang of men, say of 100 in one cutting, we have three sets of wagons going; one set at the face filling; one on the road, practically speaking, and the other at the tip discharging. If it comes on wet after ten o'clock in the morning, the men knock off, and if there is a beer-shop in the neighbourhood kept by a ganger, and if they have not money they know they have a claim upon him for the previous two or three hours they have worked, and as long as they have a claim, one or two, or three or four, of them, will insist on getting beer to the amount of what they have done.[9]

One cannot really blame the men for taking a break when the chance occurred, but it does tend to support the view of the surgeon who thought drink was responsible for accidents. It could well have been a factor in some, if not in all.

Elizabeth Garnett, who interviewed many men for her book *Our Navvies* (1885), repeated this story told to her by one of the navvies:

> I went round to Easton. We call it the slaughterhouse, you know, because every day nearly there's an accident, and nigh every week, at the farthest, a death. Well, I stood and I looked down, and there were the chaps ever so far below, and the cutting so narrow. And a lot of stone fell, it was always falling, they were bound to be hurt. There was no room to get away and mostly no warning. One chap I saw killed while I was there, anyhow he died as soon as they got him home.

Reading the parliamentary evidence of engineers and others involved in managing the construction process, one gets the impression that when accidents did occur they themselves were never at fault. The navvies were drunk, careless, inexperienced – anything except poorly supervised or put in positions of extreme danger by their overseers. There was a cavalier attitude to safety, and that same cavalier attitude was shown to any obstacles that got in the way of advancing the line. It was inevitable that where the lines had to go through urban areas there would be severe disruption to normal life, but it appears very little was done to minimise the upheaval caused to those unfortunate enough to live in the affected neighbourhoods. The line from Greenwich arrived at London Bridge after being carried on a 4-mile-long viaduct, carried on 878 arches, and one can easily imagine the chaos this caused in the area through which it was built. Bricks were brought by river from Sittingbourne in Kent to a wharf on the Surrey Canal. There were 400 men at work laying 100,000 bricks a day. It carved through an area of London that had always been poor and was described as 'the most horrible and disgusting part of the metropolis'. Cholera was raging throughout the construction period and the chaotic situation was not improved by the frequent quarrels between the two main groups of workmen. Each had their own area where they were lodged, known as English Ground and Irish Ground and it was a brave navvy who wandered into alien territory. The locals were not surprisingly deeply antagonistic to the men who had come to knock down their homes, however poor they might have been. The completion of the railway did nothing to improve the immediate neighbourhood. The promised cottages that were supposed to have been built under the arches never materialised.

Nothing it seemed was allowed to get in the way of the railway. In Leeds the line from York passed so close to the parish church that it went right through the graveyard. The headstones that had to be moved were placed on the slope of the new embankment, where they can still be seen today. Some few towns and cities were able to impose their views on the railway builders. Edinburgh insisted that the line be hidden away in a cutting, as did the genteel spa town of Harrogate. Neither was necessary in engineering terms – but the citizens were spared the vulgar sight of the trains. Perhaps few areas suffered greater disruption than London's Camden Town, when the London & Birmingham Railway was being built. The scene was described by Charles Dickens and gives a wonderfully graphic view of what the construction site looked like:

The first shock of a great earthquake had, just at the period, rent the whole neighbourhood to its centre. Traces of its course were visible on every side. Houses were knocked down; streets broken through and stopped; deep pits and trenches dug in the ground; enormous heaps of earth and clay thrown up; buildings that were undermined and shaking, propped by great beams of wood. Here, a chaos of carts, overthrown and jumbled together, lay topsy-turvy at the bottom of a steep, unnatural hill; there, confused treasures of iron soaked and rusted in something that had accidentally become a pond. Everywhere were bridges that led nowhere; thoroughfares that were wholly impassable; Babel towers of chimneys, wanting half their height; temporary wooden houses and enclosures, in the most unlikely situations; carcasses of ragged tenements and fragments of unfinished walls and arches, and piles of scaffolding and wildernesses of bricks, and giant forms of cranes, and tripods straddling above nothing. There were a hundred thousand shapes and substances of incompleteness, wildly mingled out of their places, upside down, burrowing in the earth, aspiring in the air, mouldering in the water, and unintelligible as any dream. Hot springs and fiery eruptions, the usual attendants upon earthquakes, lent their contributions of confusion to the scene. Boiling water hissed and heaved within dilapidated walls, whence, also, the glare and roar of flames came issuing forth; and mounds of ashes blocked up rights of way, and wholly changed the law and custom of the neighbourhood.

In short, the yet unfinished railroad was in progress; and, from the very core of all the dire disorder, tailed smoothly away upon its mighty course of civilization and improvement.[10]

Dickens's metaphor of a construction site as the scene of an earthquake might seem a little far-fetched, but a contemporary illustration of the scene shows something that is almost as chaotic as his colourful description suggests. He went on to describe how local entrepreneurs were already planning to make a profit out of the arrival of the railway – and were ready in the meantime to make their money from the navvies:

A brand-new tavern, redolent of fresh mortar and size, and fronting nothing at all, had taken for its sign The Railway Arms; but that might be rash enterprise – and then it hoped to sell drink to the workmen. So the Excavators' House of Call had sprung up from a beer-shop; and the old-established ham and beef shop had become the Railway Eating House, with a roast leg of pork daily, through interested motives of a similar immediate and popular description. Lodging-house keepers were favourable in like manner, and for like reason were not to be trusted.

Arguably, the most audacious example of an engineering solution to a practical problem occurred on the south coast of England between Folkestone and Dover at Round Cliff Down. That is not a name you'll be able to find even on a detailed Ordnance Survey map simply because, thanks to the arrival of the railway, it no longer exists. Can you imagine the uproar today if someone announced they were about to blow up a large section of the White Cliffs of Dover? Environmental issues did not have the same priority in the first half of the nineteenth century. When William Cubitt planned his line, it involved massive engineering works, including a 100ft-high nineteen-arch viaduct, a massive sea wall and three tunnels with a total length of over 2 miles. But Round Cliff Down was still such a problem that he decided the only solution was to blow it up. It was such a huge undertaking that the army was called in to help. Bore holes were sunk and packed with 8 tons of gunpowder, joined up by electric fuses. Word spread that this was going to be a spectacular event and the company sold tickets to those who wanted to watch the demolition of a large portion of coastal scenery. In January 1843 the big day eventually arrived: 'A dull, muffled, booming sound was heard, accompanied for a moment by a heavy jolting movement of the earth ... In an instant the bottom of the cliff appeared to dissolve.'[11] It was estimated that a million tons was spread out over some 15 acres and the company were saved £7,000 in excavation costs.

The construction of bridges and viaducts mainly used the technologies already established from the building of bridges and aqueducts on the canals. The railway age, however, demanded crossings far longer than had ever been needed in the canal age, and this called for a new approach. The engineers who designed the structures had to come up with new solutions to old problems, but the men working on site had to learn new methods and skills as well. Robert Stephenson, who was chief engineer for the important line that was to carry the Irish Mail to Holyhead, faced precisely the same problems that had confronted Telford when he was building the Holyhead Road: how to cross the estuary at Conwy and then the far greater challenge of bridging the Menai Straits to Anglesey. Telford had gone for what was then the latest available technology and built two imposing suspension bridges. They had initially been found, rather alarmingly, to sway in the wind, which may have been acceptable for a bridge designed to carry nothing bigger than a stagecoach, but was not going to be able to take a steam train. Conventional bridges built on brick or stone piers were unacceptable, simply because the waterways had to be kept clear for shipping. Stephenson's ingenious solution was to devise bridges that were huge metal tubes, with the tracks placed on the inside – in effect hollow girders – which would meet at the central pier built on the Britannia Rock in the middle of the Straits.

The tubes were constructed on site, which required as much physical exertion as digging. The heavy wrought-iron plates, as much as 3½in thick, had to be laid on weighty cast-iron blocks, known as 'stretching beds'. There they were flattened by brute force, by men yielding huge sledgehammers. Then they had to be accurately bored to take rivets. Riveting was as strenuous as the flattening process. Rivets were heated in portable stoves, usually by young boys, who pulled them out of the fire with tongs and then threw them to the riveters and those working on the top of a tube, which meant chucking them 40ft in the air. The rivet was held in place and the end hammered home. The racket of riveting those immense hollow tubes must have been all but unbearable.

The original plan had been to use conventional viaducts as approaches over the land at either end, but eventually they too were to be tubular girders. It was comparatively straightforward raising the tubes onto the supports on the land, but the four main 450ft girders that were going to span the Straits presented a far greater channel. Two of these hollow girders were joined together to form a continuous tube in which up trains could run and the other two formed the tube for down trains. Positioning them proved a nightmarish operation. They had to be floated into the correct position so they could then be jacked up into place on the towers, and this was a huge lift – the central tower built on Britannia Rock in the middle of the Straits was 230ft high. The rafts holding the first tube were to be controlled by cables attached to capstans. The tube was supposed to be edged into position opposite its mark on the Anglesey shore, but it swung past the position. The crew manning the capstan tried to stop it, but the cable jammed. Fortunately it was freed, and crowds on the shore grabbed the loose cable and, heaving with all their might, managed to prevent raft, crew and tube disappearing out to sea.

It must have seemed as if the worst of the problems had been solved. All that remained now was to bring in the heavy jacks to lift the tube into place. Stephenson was taking no chances and insisted that the tube should be followed up by supports as it was lifted. It was a wise move. The tube had just been raised a few feet when the lifting machinery failed and 50 tons of iron came crashing down, sending one of the workmen to his death. It was the last serious mishap and the bridge was eventually opened on 1 May 1848.[12]

The use of iron for bridge construction was not without its problems. Stephenson had already experienced that when a cast-iron bridge across the Dee that he had designed collapsed while a train was crossing it in 1847. The disaster marked the end of the use of cast iron for railway bridges, but worse was to follow when the wrought-iron Tay viaduct collapsed taking with it a passenger train. Ninety people lost their lives. Today, the tragedy is chiefly remembered for the wholly banal verses written for the occasion by the master of bad verse, William McGonagall. The disaster had an immediate effect. The original plans for a similar bridge across the Firth of Forth were immediately scrapped and the engineer John Fowler produced a completely new design. The new bridge would be built using steel instead of wrought iron. It is often referred to as a cantilever bridge, but might be more accurately thought of as a series of giant diamond-shaped trusses joined by girders. It is perhaps the best known of all British railway viaducts, and involved many technological innovations – and presented special problems and dangers for the men called upon to build it.

The central support was to be built on the tiny island of Inchgarvie, but this was not big enough to take the whole massive structure, so extra supports had to be installed under water. The old technology of building coffer dams was impractical in the deep waters of the Firth, so caissons had to be used instead. These were metal tubes, 70ft in diameter and the largest was 90ft high. The caissons had a sharpened lower edge, so that as they were lowered they cut through the mud and silt on the seabed until they found a firm footing. They could then be pumped out and kept clear of water by means of compressed air. Men were able to work inside the caissons, building up the foundations for the piers. It was hot, claustrophobic and thoroughly unpleasant and many men suffered from what was known as 'caisson disease'. This was in fact the equivalent of 'the bends' experienced by deep-sea divers. It was caused by men leaving the caissons too rapidly, moving from a high-pressure environment to the normal atmospheric pressure. When this happens, gas bubbles form in the blood vessels, which cause a great deal of pain and can even prove fatal.

The men who built the steel towers were mainly recruited from the heavy engineering industries of Scotland, men who were accustomed to working with steel, even if they weren't used to doing so high above the sea. They were known as 'briggers' and at the height of the construction process there were 4,000 men at work. Safety measures were virtually unknown. On such a construction site today men would have hard hats and safety harnesses. On the great bridge, they sauntered around the high scaffolding bareheaded and as nonchalantly as if they were taking a stroll down a country lane. Accidents were inevitable – a dropped rivet could fracture a man's skull. When accidents did occur, the first response of the company was to blame the men for carelessness or even drunkenness. Whatever the cause, the sad fact remains that fifty-seven men lost their lives before the job was finished. And at the end, the official report referred to the bridge as 'a wonderful example of thoroughly good workmanship'. Perhaps the briggers were not so careless after all.[13]

The accident rate and number of deaths in constructing the Forth Bridge were unusual in bridge construction. The same could not be said of working in the tunnels. This is such a big and important part of the story that it deserves a chapter to itself.

CHAPTER EIGHT

THE GREAT TUNNELS

The biggest tunnels often turned out to be nightmares for the engineers who planned them and no less nightmarish for those who had to build them. It is difficult for us to imagine what it must have been like to work in such places, but fortunately there were intrepid journalists who were prepared to go and find out and try to give their readers an idea of a working life spent underground. One of the best of these accounts describes a visit to the Box Tunnel on the Great Western between Bath and Swindon.[1]

The tunnel had to take Brunel's broad-gauge track, with rails set 7ft apart, so it had to be built to generous dimensions – 40ft high and 30ft wide – and for most of its 1¾-mile length had to be carved out of the bedrock. The anonymous journalist concentrated on a section being worked by two contractors, Lewis and Brewer, near the Chippenham end. He began by describing some of the difficulties they had faced. The biggest problem was water from underground springs, which required a steam pump working continuously to prevent flooding. But in November 1837 heavy rains proved more than the pump could cope with and the whole of the workings were flooded out, the water rising 36ft up the construction shaft. Work was stopped until the summer of the following year when the contractors brought in a second 50 horsepower pump to drain the tunnel. That winter more heavy rains came but with both pumps working flat out they were able to keep the site open. They were removing 32,000 hogsheads a day, just over 2 million gallons. To make up for lost time the contractors increased the workforce to 400 men.

The journalist visited a 1,520ft-long section of the tunnel between shafts 7 and 8. The two gangs had been working towards each other from the foot of the shafts:

> On breaking through the last intervening portion of rock the accuracy of the heading was proved and to the joy of the workmen – who took a lively interest in the result – and to the triumph of Messrs. Brewer and Lewis's scientific

working it was found that the junction was *perfectly level* the two roofs forming an unvarying line; while at the sides the utmost deviation from a straight line was only ONE INCH AND A QUARTER.

Such accuracy deserves its capital letters. Box Tunnel is in fact famous for its accurate alignment and it is said that on Brunel's birthday morning the sun shines straight through it.

The section contained a 130ft-thick band of oolitic limestone through which the tunnel had to be blasted using roughly a ton of gunpowder a week. The upside of this was that where the tunnel passed through this solid rock, no extra lining was required. Having given the readers the facts and figures, the writer went on to describe his own visit underground. It is worth quoting at length for it is probably the finest description we have of such a scene. There are accounts that contain more technical details but few that give such a good idea of the atmosphere of this underground world:

The descent by shaft No. 7, which is 136 feet deep is effected on a platform, without any railing or other security on the sides, attached to a broad flat rope wound and unwound by a steam-engine, and is attended with no inconvenience (if the idea of a fall from giddiness, or from the breaking of the rope, be not allowed to intrude) except the hard bump with which your arrival at the bottom is announced to you. The works are being carried on each way from this shaft and which, every way you go the same appearances meet you. The dark, dim vault filled with clouds of vapour is saved from utter and black darkness by the feeble light of candles which are stuck upon the sides of the excavation, and placed on trucks or other things used in carrying on the works; these, which in your immediate neighbourhood emit a dull red light are seen gradually diminishing in size and effect, till they appear like small red dots and are then lost in the dark void. Taking a candle in your hand you pick your way through pools of water over the temporary rails among blocks of stone, and the huge chains attached to the machinery which every now and then impede your way, happy and lucky if no impediment, unobserved in the dull, uncertain light should arrest your progress by causing you to measure your length on the wet and rugged floor. Pursuing your onward course, examining by the way the appearance of the works, and admiring the solid walls which nature has provided, you note every now and then a beautiful rill as clear as crystal issuing from some fissure in the rock trickling down the sides of the tunnel, and helping to form one of the many pools and streams with which the floor yet abounds. Not during all this time have your ears been idle, the sounds of the pick, the shovel, and the hammer have fallen upon them indistinctly; but as you advance they increase and the hum of distant voices is heard. The faint illumination, before only just sufficient to make darkness visible, now becomes stronger, and the light which had been placed chiefly in line along the walls becomes more frequent, they dot the whole of the opening, being pretty thickly planted from the floor to the roof. The cause for this is soon apparent: as you advance a busy scene opens before you; gangs of men are at work at all sides, and the tunnel which to this point had been cut to its full dimension, suddenly contracts; you leave the level of the floor and scrambling up among the workmen stopping sometimes on the solid rock, at others on loose fragments you wind your way slowly and with difficulty. Having been informed that a shot is about to be fired at the further extremity you stop to listen and to judge of its effects. The match is applied, the explosion follows, and a concussion such as probably you never felt before, takes place; the solid rock appears to shake and the reverberation of the sound and the shock is sensibly and fearfully experienced; another and another follow; and with a slight stretch of the imagination you may fancy yourself in the middle of a thundercloud with heaven's artillery booming around. You pursue your rugged path and having arrived at that part where the junction was made between the two cuttings, you have an opportunity of examining the roof and of admiring the solid bed of rock of which it is formed, and of appreciating the skill which enabled the engineer to keep a true course under all the difficulties of such a work. After traversing a considerable space within reach of the roof, you find your way to the bottom among a gang of labourers who are working from the other end and having arrived at the shaft at the Chippenham side of the tunnel you step upon the platform, the word is given and you are once more elevated to the surface of the earth, glad to breathe the pure air and full of wonder at the skill, enterprise and industry of your fellow-men.

What the article does not mention is that falling off the platform while being carried down the shaft was the least of the navvies' problems, as another report from about the same time makes clear:

The Great Western Railroad continues to send a great number of casualties to our infirmary and these of the most formidable description. On Monday a poor fellow was brought in with an extensive fracture of the skull from the falling of a stone from above. On Tuesday one workman with his fingers crushed: and a second, a fine lad of nineteen, most miserably mutilated; the right leg was torn entirely off and the left so shattered that Mr Morgan the surgeon of the week was obliged to separate both immediately. The unhappy sufferer bore the operation with great courage and resignation and we are happy to learn that he passed a good night! Wednesday morning early another workman was brought with a very bad compound fracture of the leg: he had fallen through a shaft 30 feet and immediate amputation was needful.[2]

Casualties seem to have been coming in on a daily basis, but occasionally even more serious incidents occurred involving several men:

A fatal accident took place on Wednesday at No. 5 shaft, Box Tunnel. As seven men were at work sinking the shaft the sides of the pit fell in killing one man on the spot; another died in the course of the day two are not expected to recover; and the other three are very much injured.[3]

Box was not the only tunnel on the line. Another accident causing fatalities was recorded at Brislington on the outskirts of Bristol:

We regret to state that one of those appalling occurrences which are almost unavoidable in public works of great momentum took place on Thursday afternoon at Brislington near this city in Tunnel No. 1 of the Great Western Railway. It seems that while some of the workmen were engaged in what is termed striking the centre of the arch; the brickwork gave way and overwhelming three of them killed them on the spot. A body of men rushed to their assistance when unfortunately a further mass gave way and seven others were injured. An inquest was held yesterday on the bodies of the deceased and a verdict of *accidental death* returned. The two wounded men who suffered most were conveyed to the Infirmary in a dangerous state.[4]

The regular reporting of accidents in the Bristol papers must have given the readers the sense that this tunnel was a decidedly dangerous place to be. The Great Western was always the most publicity conscious of all the lines and they were particularly anxious to reassure people that travelling through the tunnel was safe, whatever might have happened during construction. Unfortunately for them, a self-proclaimed expert had declared that it was potentially lethal. Dr Dionysius Lardner had a genius for predicting disasters that would occur with each advance in technology and he solemnly declared that he had worked out exactly what would happen at Box. He pointed out that the line was on a slight gradient and if the brakes were to fail when a train was on the downward run it would emerge at 120mph, a speed at which it would be impossible for human beings to breathe. Brunel merely pointed out that the good doctor's calculations paid no attention to either friction or air pressure and left it at that. Some passengers, however, were so nervous that a special coach had to be laid on in the early days to take them over Box Hill to rejoin the train on the other side. To counteract this negative approach to railway travel the company issued an illustrated book to extol the delights of travelling by train. It had a curious design: one page described the view out of one side of the carriage; the facing page the view from the opposite window.[5] As there was nothing much to be seen while going through a tunnel, the writer had to content himself with describing the approach 'with vertical sides hewn out of the rock', followed by a description of the various types of rock that the tunnel passed through, which would hardly have been visible. After that he hoped to keep the passengers amused by reciting the very impressive tunnel statistics:

The Box-tunnel is 3,195 yards, or about a mile and three-quarters long, lined nearly throughout with brickwork, and ventilated by six shafts, each 25 feet in diameter, and varying from 70 to 300 feet in depth; the whole run through it being a rapid decline westward. This tunnel, it may be interesting to know, occupied two years and a half in formation, involving the labour of excavating no less than 414,000 cubic yards of earth and stone, chiefly the latter; besides the construction of 54,000 cubic yards of masonry and brickwork, with a consumption of more than thirty million bricks. A ton of gunpowder was used weekly in blasting, and a ton of candles for lighting the labourers, who averaged more than a thousand during the whole operation.

What the writer does not mention is that it has been estimated a man lost his life for every mile of the line constructed, and around a hundred of them died at the workings under Box Hill. It seems that on this line at least they were given a dignified funeral. The Revd H.W. Lloyd, rector of Cholsey cum Moulsford, described how he conducted a ceremony for a navvy known simply as 'Happy Jack'. His old workmates turned up at the church wearing white smocks and with white ribbons in their hats and formed a procession to follow the coffin to the churchyard.

The loss of life at Box was not unique: men died wherever the great tunnels were being constructed. One of the more bizarre accidents happened at Bramhope Tunnel on the Leeds & Thirsk Railway. As at all the tunnels, work went on day and night, and one unfortunate man coming home in the dark, mistook his way, tripped and fell down an open shaft to his death: 'No one saw him fall in but heard a cry of O-dear.'[6] One cannot help feeling that the official report toned down what was heard that night; it seems likely that a tough navvy plunging down a shaft would have used somewhat stronger language. The 2-mile-long tunnel was an immense undertaking of which the company must have been proud, for its northern portal was given an elaborate Gothic treatment with towers and battlements. A miniature version of it can be seen in nearby Otley churchyard as a memorial to the twenty-three men who died during construction. Although there are some inscriptions to navvy deaths, there does not seem to be a grand memorial like this anywhere else in the country.

Although the records prove that navvies were treated in hospitals when injured, there is very little information on who paid the bills. One exception is the Northampton Infirmary, which reported that between 1835 and 1839 they

The opening of the Liverpool & Manchester railway on 15 September 1830 created a huge stir when local Member of Parliament, William Huskisson, strolled out of his carriage, failed to get off the track in time, and was run down by Rocket.

treated 124 navvies working on the nearby London & Birmingham Railway. They also noted the cost of treatment, which came to a total of £597. Of that, £115 10s was paid by the company, £10 10s by the contractors and a modest £4 11s by the men themselves. That leaves a gap of £466 9s: who made up the difference? Nothing has been noted. Looking at the history of the hospital it becomes clear that the infirmary itself paid the difference. It was founded in 1743, by public subscription, and the first annual report states: 'Here are now admitted the poor, sick, lame and no money gift or reward is taken from them or their friends on any account whatever.' In 1793 the infirmary was moved to a new, purpose-built building, and the injured navvies were fortunate in that here at least they received the best treatment available. Later reports show that the number of beds was increased specifically to take in the railway casualties. Northampton was a particularly progressive hospital: in 1847 they were using general anaesthetics just months after the first experiments in Boston, Massachusetts. Unfortunately, this was not available for the navvies who were treated here the previous decade.

The arrangements for paying for the sick varied greatly. On some construction sites sick clubs were established. Captain Moorsom, an engineer on the Chester & Holyhead Railway, recorded that on all but two of the contracts sick clubs had been established; in the case of the two exceptions no one could be persuaded to put up the money. It is unfortunately not at all clear what proportion of the funds was supplied by the men themselves and how much, if any, by the contractors. Peto was known for his generosity. In his evidence to Parliament he described how he made secret donations to the navvies' funds, paid 8 to 12s a week if a man was seriously ill and always paid compensation in case of accidents. It has to be said that only a few contractors followed his example.

The most demanding of all the tunnels in the first decades of railway construction was bored through the heart of the Pennines. It was built by the Sheffield, Ashton-under-Lyne & Manchester Railway and took its name from that of the nearest village to the site, Woodhead. Everything about the operation was daunting. For a start there was the length – just over 3 miles – and it had to be carved out of rock. The most challenging aspect of all was its situation. The construction site was on rough moorland, 1,500ft above sea level. Woodhead itself was nothing more than a hamlet and the nearest town of any size was miles away. As anyone who has ever spent much time in the Pennines will know, the weather at these heights can be fierce at any time of the year and can feel positively arctic in winter. I can all too clearly remember setting off on a walk one winter's day after a modest snowfall and finding the combination of the tufted grasses and snowdrifts almost impossible to get through, and abandoning the enterprise in favour of a pint by a pub fire. The navvies who came here would not have had the luxury of a local pub to call in on, and I can scarcely imagine what it must have been like to live here in the wretched accommodation that they had to endure. The story of Woodhead is dramatic, part heroic epic and partly a shoddy tale of greed and misery.

Problems appeared from the very start and the way in which they were dealt with impacted on everyone involved in the project. The Act was approved in 1835 and the company set about hiring a chief engineer. The two main applicants were Joseph Locke and Charles Vignoles, and the job went to the latter. Vignoles had an interesting and unusual early career. He had started out as an army officer, but in 1917, like many other peacetime officers, was retired on half pay; as he had no private income he had to go and try to find work. His first idea was to use his professional expertise by volunteering to join Simon Bolivar's army and he set sail for America. He never got beyond South Carolina, where he managed to get himself appointed as assistant to the state engineer. From there he moved on to Florida as city surveyor for St Augustine. He returned to England just in time for the start of the great boom in railway construction. His first job was on the Liverpool & Manchester Railway under George Stephenson, where he was involved with work on the Edge Hill Tunnel. He got off on the wrong foot with Stephenson from the first, and when things went wrong at the tunnel Stephenson had the perfect excuse to sack him. Vignoles's own version of his experience is decidedly interesting. Stephenson notoriously disliked 'London men' and he had already quarrelled with Josias Jessop, the engineer who had been called in to consult on the works. Vignoles was next:

> I also acknowledge having on many occasions differed with him (and that in common with almost all other engineers) because it appeared to me he did not look on the concern with a liberal and expanded view, but with a microscopic eye; magnifying details, and pursuing a petty system of parsimony, very proper in a private colliery, or in a small undertaking, but wholly inapplicable to this national work.
>
> I also plead guilty to having neglected to court Mr. S's favour by crying down all other engineers, especially those in London, for, though I highly respect his great natural talents, I could not shut my eyes to certain deficiencies.[7]

Vignoles would have known that Stephenson had, in fact, been highly sceptical about the whole project and promised to eat the first locomotive that came through the tunnel. The temptation to go one better than the great man must have been irresistible. At the start he set out precisely what he meant to do and how he meant to do it in a report that was a model of lucidity.[8] First he stressed a need for a survey to be carried out, 'with geometrical accuracy', after which the process of acquiring the land could continue. In the meantime, he would start on the tunnel. He proposed sinking eleven shafts, evenly spread along the line, the deepest of which would be approximately 600ft. He had checked with local lead miners in Derbyshire and calculated it would cost

£500 per shaft, not including the cost of pumping engines. He was sure sinking could proceed at a rate of 7 yards a week, given a competent workforce:

> I conceive there will be no difficulty in finding in the Country as many Gangs of Working Miners as will enable the whole number of shafts to be worked at once; first building huts on the Hills for the men; a measure absolutely necessary for the absence of all accommodation for them otherwise.

In fact, he took a very cautious approach. In order to move things forward as rapidly as possible he decided to construct a tunnel just wide enough to take a single-track line. He was well aware that there was a shortage of cash in hand but the Act allowed the company to call on shareholders for extra money when it was needed, which they were legally obliged to provide. He was quite certain that when the shareholders saw how well things were progressing, there would be no problems. Everything sounded perfect in theory: practice was to prove very different.

Work began in 1838 and things soon started to go badly wrong. The weather was atrocious and Vignoles's 7 yards a week proved totally unattainable. Things were made even worse by the company's reluctance to release funds for anything at all other than absolute necessities. Huts for the men did not fall into that category. At first the men simply slept rough wherever they could find somewhere reasonably dry and comfortable. It was not a situation that could be endured for long, and eventually Vignoles persuaded the company to act. But instead of constructing huts, they sent tents. These were never going to be enough to see the men through a harsh Pennine winter, so they took matters into their own hands, building rough shelters from whatever material they could find.

Confidence in the company had never been high among investors and Vignoles agreed to buy shares himself. A feature of railway shares was that they were not a one-off investment: the Act of Parliament gave the company the right to call on shareholders for extra funds. Vignoles bought his shares on the clear understanding that this was a way of helping out the company in their hour of need and that he would not be required to pay on future calls. For a time the share value plummeted and when it rose Vignoles decided to hold on to his shares as a mark of confidence in the project. He was an honourable man who had not realised that the Board of Directors were not equally scrupulous. In spite of earlier promises, when cash became short again he was called on to put in extra funds. He did not have the money. Lord Wharncliffe, the chairman, who had made the gentleman's agreement with Vignoles, did his best to persuade the directors that they should honour it. They simply refused. Vignoles

Sudden collapses and landslips represented a real danger to the navvies.

held £100,000 in shares, which he could have sold when the market was high; the best deal he was offered now was to sell and salvage what he could. He lost £80,000 on the deal and left the company, writing in his diary: 'Good God, that men whom I had served so faithfully and for whose railway I had done so much, should act like this.' Lord Wharncliffe also did the honourable thing and left in disgust at the treatment Vignoles had received. In time, Vignoles would recover his fortune and enjoy a successful career. In the meantime, Locke took over the works. Throughout the construction period, the reluctance – and often inability – of the company to come up with money, and their taking the view that costs must always be driven down, was to affect everyone who worked in the great tunnel.

Vignoles had originally estimated the total cost of the tunnel at £60,000; this had now risen to £200,000. Locke's first action was to get rid of the small contractors who had been working on the tunnel and replace them with just two men: Richard Hattersley at the western end and Thomas Nicholson at the east. Originally there had been about 400 men at work and there needed to be more than twice as many for the work to go forward at the sort of rate that would appease the shareholders. When work had started labour had been every bit as plentiful as Vignoles had suggested it would be. Now, with new works starting all over the country, this was no longer the case. Given a choice of sites a man had to be desperate to come to Woodhead, with its appalling conditions and wretched accommodation. As a result, the contractors had to take whatever they could get – and even then had to pay more than was being offered on other railway sites. With rising costs, the engineer on the spot, Wellington Purdon, had to cut costs wherever he could.

Purdon was one of the few engineers who had worked his way up from the very bottom of the ladder. He had started out as a labourer on the Stockton & Darlington and you didn't rise as far as he had done by being a soft touch. Safety was definitely not high on his list of priorities. Woodhead was notorious for the high accident rate, and Purdon was questioned about the issue when he gave his evidence to the 1846 Committee. The initial discussion centred on the method used in 'stemming', ramming the gunpowder charge into the drilled hole. There was a body of opinion that many accidents were caused because an iron rod was used, which if it hit the rock wall could create a spark that would ignite the powder. The committee quoted an example from Woodhead: 'William Jackson, miner, No. 5 shaft. He was looking over John Webb's shoulder, while he was stemming a hole charged with powder, when the blast went off, blowing the stemmer through Jackson's head, and killed him on the spot.'

Was it not true, the committee asked, that accidents such as this could be avoided by using a copper stemmer instead of one made of iron? Purdon totally dismissed the suggestion: copper stemmers were too soft to do the job properly. They were also – though he did not mention the fact – more expensive.

By this time the safety fuse had come into use. It had been invented by Samuel Bickford who lived in Cornwall and it was originally used in the local tin and copper mines. It consisted of a cord, with one central thread saturated with gunpowder. He invented a machine for manufacturing the fuse to ensure consistency, so that it could be relied on always to burn at a consistent rate. This meant that the time between lighting the fuse and the actual explosion could be calculated with a good deal of accuracy and could be set so that men could clear the site. Many railway engineers adopted it and one of them, Captain Moorsom of the Chester & Holyhead line, became a passionate advocate of the new system. Purdon remained wholly unimpressed. The committee asked Purdon if he ever used safety fuses. He did not. But, they persisted, was it not much safer? He replied: 'Perhaps it is; but it is attended with such a loss of time, and the difference is so very small, I would not recommend the loss of time for the sake of the extra lives it would save.' As there was nothing he was prepared to do to prevent accidents, could he perhaps persuade the company to offer compensation? That idea too was rejected: the company, he said, were not interested and neither were the contractors. It is small wonder that men were reluctant to work at Woodhead.

There are no accurate records of how many died during the work at Woodhead, but the doctor Henry Lacey Pomfret recorded twenty-three compound fractures, seventy-four simple fractures and 140 miscellaneous injuries including burning and blinding. There was a sick club, and one contractor at least showed appropriate compassion. Thomas Nicholson described the arrangements for burying the dead:

> A good oak coffin, provided at my expense, and the person at his death, if he had friends, was given up to them, to be interred wherever they thought proper, the club paying the expenses. If they had no friends they were buried either at Penistone or Woodhead; and I have heard the public remark their entire satisfaction of the way in which these men were interred. The usual allowance for parties attending the funeral is a dinner and one quart of ale.[9]

There were, he said, 'no instances of any misconduct at a funeral'. There was one exception, apparently, in the case of William Lee, who died in January 1842. He was walking with his head down on a windy day when he was hit in the chest by the arm of the horse gin. He fractured his spine. He lay, suffering, for many days, pleading for a clergyman to come to him to read the scriptures and offer him comfort. No one came. This became well known in the navvy community, so the anger of those who came to his funeral is hardly surprising. Dr Pomfret who reported on injuries also gave evidence to the Parliamentary Committee on his experiences in trying to get the clergy to visit a dying man. He reported a very similar case to that of Lee's of a dying navvy asking in vain for a clergyman to come to his bedside. Pomfret was questioned in detail about the circumstances:

How near does the clergyman reside to the place where this man lay?

– Nine miles. I think the neglect may be attributed to this circumstance, there was some little disagreement about the district.

Do the clergymen ever think it their duty to attend?

– I conveyed this message about this man myself to the clergyman, and he said he would attend, and I borrowed a horse for him, but he never availed himself of it.

Did you ever hear what reason was assigned for his not attending in the case you alluded to?

– Engagements about home, I believe.

The result was this man went without?

– The result was that I went to a Methodist and offered him a day's wages to go, and the man died before he got to the house.

The clergy were loud in their condemnation of the irreligious navvies. The navvies would have been quite within their rights to make the same accusation against clergy who squabbled about which parish a man was actually dying in and then did not turn up to see him.

The first tunnel was completed in 1845 and two years later work began on a second tunnel to take the next track and that was completed in 1852. The working conditions at Woodhead were always atrocious and the living conditions were little better. How the men lived, how they were provided with the essentials of life and what the world thought about them will be dealt with in the next chapter. Many of the miseries they endured both on and off work were directly attributed to the difficulties of the task and the nature of the immediate surroundings. These combined to make Woodhead notorious as one of the worst, if not *the* worst, worksites throughout the history of railway construction in Britain. There was to be one tunnel, however, that offered the greatest engineering challenge of them all.

The River Severn had always proved an obstacle to communication between England and South Wales. Telford had constructed a road bridge across the river at Gloucester, but below that everyone had to rely on ferries. The Great Western had been discussing the idea of a tunnel near Bristol for some years: it would cut an hour off the journey time from Paddington to Cardiff. They were given the appropriate Act in 1872, but progress was painfully slow for the next few years. It was the opening of a ¾-mile-long iron bridge across the river at Sharpness in 1879, which gave their rival, the Midland, better access to South Wales, that spurred them into action. The job of constructing the tunnel was eventually handed to Sir John Hawkshaw who, as soon as he became chief engineer, appointed Thomas Walker as principal contractor. The latter was persuaded to write a book about the work which, he declared, 'proved to me a more arduous task than a year's superintendence of the Tunnel itself'. His job was not made any easier by poor health and he was to die a year after the work was published at the age of sixty-one. Hawkshaw wrote of him in a preface to a later edition:

Mr. Walker's practice of going into all the details of his works himself brought upon him an immense amount of labour over and above that which must necessarily fall to the lot of a large contractor, and it probably tended to shorten his life … I know of no contractor who has displayed so much care and solicitude for the comfort and welfare of the workpeople by him, as Mr. Walker.

Those words seem to have been no more than he deserved. Walker may have found writing a chore but he left us one of the most complete accounts that we have of the technical and other difficulties faced by everyone involved in such work. All the quotes that follow are taken from his book.[10]

The challenge was immense. The only comparable venture had been Marc Brunel's tunnel under the Thames, but that had been intended for pedestrians and carriages and was accessed by a spiral ramp at either end. The trains using the Severn Tunnel would have to take a far more gentle approach. There would need to be cuttings at either end to ease the way to the tunnel portals and the tunnel itself would have to be built on two gradients, sloping down from either end to meet at a level section 200ft below the starting points. The whole excavations would cover 7 miles, including 4½ miles of tunnel of which 2 miles would be beneath the river itself.

Work began in 1872, with the sinking of an exploratory shaft on the west bank of the river. There was a village some distance away, but the only building near the site was a farmhouse called Sudbrook and this was to become the centre of operations that would eventually become the focus of a small town. It began with the construction of a small office and half a dozen cottages for the men. The first shaft was a major undertaking, 15ft in diameter and 200ft deep, eventually known as the 'Old Shaft'. From here, headings were driven of quite modest dimensions, just 7ft square. By 1877 they had reached out towards the river for 1,600 yards and by then small contracts had been let out to extend the work and a second shaft intended to be the main pumping shaft was begun. Then on 18 October disaster struck. The workers hit what was always referred to afterwards as the Great Spring and water poured through into the tunnel. Fortunately the men were just changing shifts. As the water cascaded down from a drop of 40ft to flood the Old Shaft, the men were able to make their way to the new shaft and safety. Valiant efforts were made to stem the flood but within twenty-four hours the water had reached river level. Five years' work was submerged. It was at this point that Hawkshaw, who had been retained as consultant engineer, was appointed as chief engineer, and his one condition was that he should select the contractor – he chose Walker. Hawkshaw explained why he was the first choice. Walker had been the contractor on the East London Railway extension from Wapping to Shadwell, which had to pass right under London Docks. This had been a most difficult work but had proved a great success and demonstrated that the contractor had experience of tunnelling beneath deep water. Apart from acquiring the services of Walker himself, he also had the satisfaction of knowing that the contractor planned to bring some of his best men with him to the new project.

Work now moved forward at a far brisker pace. It was obvious that big pumps were going to be needed and the shafts needed to be closed off. Walker decided the best way to reopen the workings was by constructing heavy oak shields to close off the shafts. The trouble was they could only be positioned by divers working at the bottom of the shaft, who had to arrange a system of signals with the men above, who controlled the machinery used to lower the doors into the tunnel. With three pumps working, the divers went down: 'The depth of water from the shield to the surface being about 140 feet, the pressure upon the divers was so great that very few men were able to bear it at all, and no man could do work requiring great physical exertion under that pressure.'

The work was never easy. Pumps kept breaking down and the efforts of the divers to repair them underwater were hazardous in the extreme. One of the divers in particular, a man called Lambert, did a tremendous job, but at one point he was sucked into the grill at the bottom of the pump pipe and it took three men with ropes to pull him clear.

Keeping the workings clear of water required enormous power. One pumping house was a permanent fixture and contained six steam engines made by the famous Cornish manufacturers Harvey of Hayle, each with a cylinder that was 70in in diameter and 12ft long. As well as these monsters, several temporary smaller pumps were in use. Gradually, the job of clearing the workings of water progressed, but a point was reached when it was essential to close off a door that had been left open by the men racing to escape the earlier flood. It was to be another job for a diver, but although he would only be working under 30ft of water, he had to walk for 1,000ft, dragging his heavy air hose behind him:

As it was impossible for one diver to drag so long a length of hose as 1,000 feet after him up the heading, three divers were engaged. One stood at the bottom of the shaft to pass the hose, which was a floating hose, round the end from the shaft into the heading; the two others then started up the heading for a distance of 500 feet, where one remained to pull forward the hose and feed it to the leading diver.

The leading man, in whom I had thorough confidence, was named Lambert. He started on his perilous journey armed with only a short iron bar, and carefully groped his way in total darkness over the *débris* which strewed the bottom of the heading, past upturned skips, tools, and lumps of rock, which had been left in the panic of 1879, until he reached 100 feet from the door, when he found it was impossible to drag the air-hose after him, as it rose to the top of the heading, and its friction against the rock and the head-trees offered greater resistance than he could overcome. He, however, would not give up without an effort, and he pluckily sat down and drew some of the hose to him and then started on again, but after one or two vain efforts he found it impossible to proceed, and was obliged to return to the shaft defeated.

Walker, however, had heard about a patent diving suit invented by a gentleman called Fleuss, which used compressed air in a 'knapsack' on the diver's back instead of a hose to the surface. Fleuss brought his suit to the site but proved a hopelessly inexpert diver. There was only one thing to do: call on Lambert again and get him to try the new device. Walker warned him of the dangers: if he caught the knapsack and ruptured it his air supply would be gone. It was an anxious time. Lambert disappeared down the shaft and was away for an hour and twenty minutes. When he returned showing, Walker said, no sign of exhaustion, he was able to announce the work had been done: the door was closed. There is no mention of any special award to Lambert for his exceptional courage, but at least Walker was unstinting in his praise.

On the whole, the working relationship between Walker and the men was good, but there were some who it seems harboured a grudge. Before he took over they had worked eight-hour shifts, but he changed it to ten, although they twice came out of the tunnel for meals. There was a good reason for this. When a shot was fired, the tunnel filled with dangerous fumes, as they were now using gun-cotton instead of black powder, so Walker had shots fired just before meal breaks to allow time for the fumes to clear. As a result of this arrangement, they actually worked for just seven of the ten hours for which they were paid. Some, however, were not satisfied and went on strike, demanding a return to the eight-hour system. They were not perhaps anticipating Walker's response. In his own words, he said: 'My good men, you will never get that, if you stop here for a hundred years. There is a train at two o'clock, and if you don't make haste and get your money you will lose your train. You had better get your money as soon as you can and go.'

The works were stopped for four days, but Walker was happy that he had got rid of troublemakers. With new men the work proceeded at a good pace. There were a few scares: the threat of flooding was never far from anyone's mind. At one point all the men came up declaring that the river had broken in, but it turned out to be a false alarm. There was a sense that everything was going well but on 10 October 1883 the Great Spring broke through again. In the words of the ganger, 'the water broke in from the heading, rolling up all at once like a great horse'. The men were swept off their feet and three were drowned; the rest managed to fight their way out through the flood. The pumps went to work and soon men were back down in the tunnel, repairing the damage. Then on the night of 17 October a gale was blowing from the south-west and it coincided with an exceptionally high tide. The result was a tidal wave that swept over Sudbrook, flooding the houses and cascading down the shaft. One or two men who were at the bottom of the shaft managed to escape, but one man was halfway up the ladder when he was washed away and died. Eighty-three men were trapped but managed to make their way to stagings above the floodwaters. A rescue party was quickly formed and a boat lowered down the shaft. The men in the boat found their way blocked by timbers, but eventually they were able to saw their way through to reach the trapped men. All were rescued.

The Severn Tunnel was finally opened to traffic on 1 December 1886. The pumps still had to be kept in daily use, removing between 23 and 30 million gallons a day. It had been an immense task, which at its busiest had employed over 3,000 men, whose pay ranged from 8s 4d a day for foremen to between 3s 4d and 4s 2d a day for the labourers; at the bottom of the list were over 200 boys, some of them earning no more than 2d a day. In the course of the work there were inevitably fatalities and injuries, but Walker was proud of his safety record and at least those who were injured had immediate access to help. Sudbrook had become a small town complete with its own hospital, mission hall and coffee house, but not, it seems, a pub. The men who worked on the tunnel seem to have been treated fairly, enjoyed decent accommodation and good facilities. Many other railway workers would have regarded Sudbrook as almost a navvy heaven – except, of course, for the absence of a pub.

CHAPTER NINE

LIFE ON THE LINE

Navvies may have been defined by the work they did, but that was not the whole story. They did, indeed, work prodigiously hard, but not for twenty-four hours a day, seven days a week. Like everyone else, they had to take time off to eat, sleep and whenever possible enjoy themselves. The first priority was to find somewhere to live. This was easiest when the work took them through heavily populated areas, but they always faced problems. Locals tended to regard them with suspicion from the first. When the South Staffordshire Railway was constructing its line through Rushall, the farmers in the parish asked the JP to swear in a special constable to protect their property. Their appeal contained examples of the problems they were already facing: 'the first week they came into the neighbourhood I lost a couple of ducks.' The complaints hardly suggest a major crime wave and even though one farmer complained that there were several hundred navvies 'about my premises at night', the worst he could accuse them of was that 'they pull my straw places about'.[1]

Getting accommodation was never easy and it is difficult to discover exactly what sort of lodging many navvies found. One town about which we do have positive information is Knaresborough in Yorkshire, simply because a census was taken in 1851 at the time the East & West Riding Junction Railway was under construction. This was a busy site as the line had to cross the deep valley of the River Nidd on a high, stone viaduct. It is one of the more picturesque structures on the railway system, being decked out with mock medieval turrets and crenellations to mirror the nearby ruined castle. The census shows that a quarter of the men were locals, a quarter Irish and the rest from all over the country. Knaresborough is a small market town, but like all towns with regular markets there was no shortage of pubs and provisions, which was good news for the workforce. Although there was a shortage of lodging houses, the locals did their best to profit from the sudden influx of workers by cramming in as many navvies as they could manage. One family, with four children of their own, was living in what was described as an agricultural cottage. Somehow they managed to find space for nineteen lodgers, including four married couples and three children. In general, the English found it easier to find rooms than the Irish, but one Irish widow took in seventeen lodgers.[2]

The same problems recurred all round Britain and more details of living conditions emerge from the evidence given to the 1846 Committee. There were estimated to be over 2,000 Scots and Irish working in the Edinburgh area in the early 1840s. Again it was the Scots who were able to get lodgings, while the Irish had to make do with wooden huts, roofed with turf, that were put up by the contractor. The huts were approximately 20ft by 10ft, divided into two rooms with a central fireplace. They were filled with tiers of bunk beds and there were usually two or three to a bed. They held anything from twenty to thirty people, and that could include wives and children. No regular pattern emerges, with every line seeming to have different arrangements for finding homes for the men they employed. Some navvies were provided with comparatively good accommodation, especially when a conscientious contractor such as Peto was in charge. He arranged to have barracks built, with 'a steady married man' in charge, whose wife did the cooking. The single men paid a shilling a week to sleep in hammocks, and there were separate arrangements for married men. Not everyone, however, appreciated such 'luxury'. Captain Moorsom described what happened when he was resident engineer on the Chester & Holyhead. The company provided sound 'wooden huts, with slated roofs; but the Welsh, who compose a large proportion of the labourers, do not like them, as they say, because they are too fine'.

As the army of navvies settled into whatever accommodation they could find, the nervous locals waited for the worst to happen. The village of Kilsby near Rugby was all but overwhelmed when over 1,000 men descended on it to work on a tunnel on the London & Birmingham Railway. Like so many other tunnels it was to present the engineer, Robert Stephenson, with enormous challenges. There were the usual problems, with water flooding the works that required continuous pumping and when the water was conquered, they hit quicksands. The work fell seriously behind schedule and the navvies worked flat out night and day, encouraged by the engineer. 'Robert Stephenson infused into the workmen so much of his own energy that when either of their companions were killed by their side they merely threw the body out of sight and forgot his death in their own exertions.'[3]

In his evidence, the engineer Robert Rawlinson explained how the men were lodged: some found lodgings and the company built sixty brick cottages but the rest had to make do with living in huts. He described the squalid conditions:

If they had been looked after by the men themselves, they were respectable, well-built, good-sized huts; but there was no sort of superintending control over them; the men crowded them as much as they chose; one man would take a room and let it out, or sublet it to others; and they got filthy and dirty, and abounded with vermin … fever and small-pox broke out amongst them.

Even those who did get lodgings were little better off:

Besides the 1250 labourers employed in the construction of the tunnel, a proportionate number of suttlers and victuallers of all descriptions concentrated in the village of Kilsby. In several houses there lodged in each room 16 navvies, and as there were four beds in each apartment, two navvies were consequently in each, the two squads of 8 men alternately changing places with each other as in their work.[4]

The word 'suttler' may be unfamiliar to readers. The dictionary defines it as one who follows armies to sell provisions, which makes it very appropriate for these followers of the navvy armies.

When they did get time off, these hard men were not likely to want to settle for a quiet time in the overcrowded filthy accommodations described by Rawlinson and others. Instead they headed off for The Ox Green pub at Kilsby where, according to Lord of the Manor Charles Bracebridge, they rolled beer barrels out on to the village green and proceeded to raise hell. There were dog fights and cockfights on which a week's wages could be lost. When they were hungry they would buy a whole animal from a local farmer, carve it up on the village green and roast it on the spot. Fights were commonplace and the villagers, who had been used to a quiet country life, were terrified. Eventually they lost patience with the riotous behaviour and contrived to capture two of the most belligerent navvies and take them to the lockup. They were not there long before their mates broke in and released them. Finally the authorities stepped in and sixteen men were arrested and marched away to Daventry gaol. No one would have wanted to be a resident of Kilsby while the navvies were there but, in spite of the uproar, drunkenness and squabbling, the navvies seem to have done far more damage to each other than they did to anyone else. More serious trouble could erupt when the navvies found themselves in an area where there were large numbers of other, equally belligerent workers. That is what appears to have happened at Preston in Lancashire in 1838.

The whole affair began with what should have been a minor disagreement. Two Irish navvies from the North Union Railway had been refused credit at a local shop, and blamed another navvy for having turned their shopkeeper against them. They decided he was hiding out in a local cottage and when they found no trace of him, they smashed everything in sight and left in a foul temper, heading for the pub. That might have been the end of the matter, but the local Bashall cotton mill had been temporarily closed down due to an accident and a number of the local weavers were also in the pub. The two men joined their fellow navvies who had just been paid and were drinking heavily. The two angry men were by now convinced that it was the locals who were hiding the navvy they blamed for their troubles. Others joined in the argument and it ended with a confrontation between the navvies and the weavers. The Irish appear to have challenged the weavers to a fight and the weavers left, but soon returned with all kinds of clubs and gave the Irish a beating. Things now became even worse. The Irish went back to their camp to get reinforcements and marched back into town, attacking anyone they met. According to the local paper, two carters, who had nothing to do with the quarrel, were so badly beaten that it was thought they were unlikely to recover. Meanwhile, the weavers had been joined by local agricultural workers. The magistrates stepped in and separated the two parties, but it proved no more than a temporary truce. The Preston paper carried a full report of what happened next:

> Both parties determined to fight it out, and accordingly they armed themselves with guns, pistols, pikes, and other weapons, and assembling to the number of about eight hundred near the house of a man named Smith, had a regular fight. One man named John Trafford was shot through the body with slugs, and after walking a few yards fell down and expired. Several of the Englishmen received dangerous gunshot wounds. Two Irishmen are at present in the Preston Infirmary, one named Cassidy, and the other Kavanagh. One of them has had both his arms broken by a gunshot. A man named Bacon Dale received three gunshot wounds, one of which (through his loins) it is believed has entered his bladder. He is past the hope of recovery. A man named William Robinson received a gunshot wound in the arm and had his skull fractured. He is not expected to recover. The Irishmen deny having carried fire-arms, but it is rather a curious circumstance that six or eight Englishmen should have been shot if the opposite party had not carried fire-arms. It is believed that upwards of twenty Irishmen have been severely, if not dangerously wounded, but few of the belligerent parties dare come forward to give their evidence in a proper manner. These doings having been made known to the magistrates, a party of the 86th Regiment of foot were sent from Blackburn, and they arrived after all the mischief was over.[5]

It is worth repeating that such events made headlines in the press but were comparatively rare. It is doubtful that a large body of navvies settling on a town or village ever passed placid, peaceful lives, but the main problem was drunkenness and when fights did break out it was mainly among themselves. They were inevitably scapegoats for any crimes committed while they were in the area. When there was an outbreak of sheep stealing near the Bramhope Tunnel, suspicion inevitably fell on the navvies, but the local police inspector turned out to be a sleuth in the best tradition: 'I know a gang of disreputable characters at Horsforth and from traces of footsteps, the lengths of footsteps, the way in which the sheep are killed, and other circumstances, I am satisfied the Horsforth thieves are the parties committing these depredations, and not your workpeople.'[6]

Many lines had major construction sites far from any habitation. It is easy for us to forget how wild much of Britain was in the nineteenth century and that some lines passed through countryside that was not served by even the most basic roads. One story in particular gives a wonderful picture of what it meant to venture out into the wilderness. One of the most scenic railway lines in the British Isles runs from Glasgow to Fort William. Travelling the train today, the scenery is still wild and on some sections you are as likely to catch sight of a fine Scottish stag as you are to see another human being. Wildest of all is Rannoch Moor. It might look beautiful from the comfort of a railway carriage but, as anyone who has ever walked there will know, it can be a nightmarish terrain of peaty bogs and tough tussocks of grass and heather, with no shelter to be had anywhere. This was the ground that had to be conquered by the men who came here to build a railway.

The first essential step was to survey the route. The party who were to walk the route decided to do so in January, when Highland weather is notoriously unpredictable. The group consisted of the contractor Robert McAlpine, three engineers, two land agents and a solicitor. The only precaution taken against bad weather was ludicrous: two of the party carried umbrellas. The first part of the journey went according to plan, going by coach to Inverlair Lodge where they had been assured a guide would be waiting. No guide appeared so they set off on foot to the end of Loch Teig. They arrived at dusk and found a waiting boatman and a very leaky boat, which they had to bail water out of using their boots. They could at least console themselves that they had been promised a literally warm welcome at the other end of the 5-mile-long loch: a blazing fire, a hot meal and comfortable beds at Lord Abinger's hunting lodge. No one was there: no fires were lit, no meals prepared.

It might have been wiser to abandon the whole expedition at that point but they decided to march on across the wildest part of the moor on a 23-mile trek under lowering skies. This is energy-sapping country for walkers. John Brett, a sixty-year-old local factor, was the first to fail and the two brollies proved useful as a makeshift tent. McAlpine decided to set off to look for help and disappeared on his own into the gloom. Bullock, one of the engineers, also decided to see if he could find assistance and wandered off. As the light faded, he tripped over and knocked himself out. On coming round he found he had stumbled over a fence

The reputation of the navvies was so widespread that on at least one occasion they found a way of increasing their earnings by acting as a hired mob to intimidate voters.

and argued, quite reasonably, that if he followed the fence it was bound to lead somewhere; sure enough, he eventually located a shepherd's hut. Two shepherds set off and found Brett, huddled under the brollies and half dead with cold. McAlpine, meanwhile, had managed to keep to the correct route and ended up in civilisation. The whole party had finally reached safety and the entire route had been travelled, albeit partly in the dark. It was as well they finished when they did: the next day a blizzard struck and they could easily have died of exposure. The story is bizarre and although it does not involve any navvies, it does give an indication of the sort of terrain over which they would have to work and in which they would have to make their temporary homes. Other parts of the country would prove equally hostile.

A brief mention was made in the last chapter of the pathetic attempt by the railway company to provide accommodation for the workers at the Woodhead Tunnel by handing out tents. In the end, the men had to look after themselves and put together their own huts:

> The huts are a curiosity. They are mostly made of stones without mortar; the roof of thatch or of flags, erected by the men for their own temporary use, one workman building a hut in which he lives with his family, and lodges also a number of his fellow workmen. In some instances as many as fourteen or fifteen men ... Many of the huts were filthy dens, while some were whitewashed and more cleanly.[7]

The conditions must have been atrocious, especially in winter when the wind would have whistled through the gaps in the dry stone walls. One man recorded having to dig a path through 4ft of snow, just to get to work. The surgeon who visited the men seemed less concerned with the physical conditions in which the men lived than with their moral character. They were 'excessively drunken and dissolute – that a man would sell his wife to a neighbour for a gallon of beer – that a large proportion of both sexes [more than half, he stated] laboured under some form of syphilitic disease'. Comments such as these were common from those who troubled to report on how the men lived: poor overcrowded huts, with families and single men sharing rooms; as one of them put it, 'a humane man would hardly put a pig in them'. But no one did very much about it.

Some of the most extreme conditions were experienced on a line that no one really wanted to build, the Settle & Carlisle Railway. It was born out of the mishmash of routes begun in the early years of railway construction. At the southern end, it started with an extension of the Leeds & Bradford Railway to Skipton in 1849. This was taken over by the Midland Railway in 1851. It was later pushed further north as far as Ingleton. It was intended to link with the Lancaster & Carlisle Railway, opened in 1861, which to add to the confusion was actually worked by the North Western Railway (NWR). They too built a line south to Ingleton, which should have made for a convenient through route. The trouble was that the two lines finished up at stations a mile apart, separated by a viaduct. The NWR did not encourage through running, so the Midland, anxious to have a good connection with Scotland and the north of England, applied for an Act for a more direct route from Settle Junction to Carlisle. Surveying began in 1865 but a financial crisis brought everything to a halt. Four years later, when the economic climate had improved, the Midland decided they didn't want the line after all, but it was too late. Parliament insisted that as funds had been raised the line must be built. Reluctantly the company went ahead. Railway enthusiasts, at least, can be grateful as it is a gloriously scenic line, passing through some of the most remote and rugged parts of the Dales. It is all gloriously picturesque for those who travel along the line, but it is precisely this landscape that presented such a challenge to those who had to build it.

To describe the terrain as difficult for railway builders is a huge understatement. There are areas of peaty bog in some parts and boulder clay in others. At Batty Moss, the worst of the bogs, moving material was especially difficult and carts had to have their normal narrow wheels replaced with barrels to stop them sticking. The going was so tough that sometimes as many as three horses were needed for each cart, and even then they were likely to sink into the mire and had to be rescued. The boulder clay provided a very different challenge. This is a particularly solid clay, often mixed with stones and even, as its name suggests, boulders; it was so hard that in dry weather it had to be blasted away. However, dry weather was a luxury in these parts, high in the hills, with many parts of the line being built at an altitude of over 1,000ft, the actual summit at Ais Gill being at 1,150ft. In the winter season of 1872, 72in of rain fell at Dent Head, the site of the present Dent station. When it did rain heavily the clay turned to a gooey mess. It was not only painfully difficult to dig, oozing off the spade, but when it had been loaded into trucks, it refused to come out again. The trucks were tipped, but the clay was stuck fast inside. It was small wonder that many of the navvies faced with such conditions soon left. In May 1871 records showed 6,980 men at work, but as the rain poured down and work became impossible, 1,000 walked away. It was estimated that altogether over 30,000 navvies came to the Settle & Carlisle, though there was never more than a quarter of that number at work at any one time. As one of the engineers ironically remarked, 'they do like a change'.

There were major engineering works on the line, including a 2,650-yard tunnel at Blea Moor and nineteen viaducts. The most impressive of the latter was at Ribblehead, carried at a height of over 150ft above the valley on twenty-four stone arches. The most demanding work was inevitably in the least hospitable part of the line, and it was here that the familiar problem of finding somewhere to stay became particularly acute. It is, incidentally, a measure of just how remote the line was that even when completed, Dent station was 4 miles away from the actual village of Dent.

The first party arrived on site during the winter of 1869/70. The men in charge had a hut on wheels, known as 'The Contractors Hotel' and the men had to make do with tents pitched on Blea Moor – Bleak Moor would have been an equally appropriate name. In the spring, men began to pour on to the site and by the summer of 1870 there were a hundred huts spread out along the line. They were generally of a far higher quality than the ones put up by the navvies at Woodhead, built of timber and covered in roofing felt. That did not prevent the familiar scenario of overcrowding. The medical officer of health from Sedbergh described one hut where the beds were so closely crowded together that the only way to reach the ones furthest from the door was to clamber over the rest.

As settlements became more permanent they were given names. It is probable that at least some of the navvies had been over to the Crimea (see Chapter Eleven) as two of the settlements were called Sebastopol and Inkerman. Quite how Jericho and Jerusalem got their names is a mystery, but it must have been a navvy with a wry sense of humour who described a huddle of huts in a quagmire as Belgravia. However bizarre the names may have been, they were given official recognition in the parish register at Chapel le Dale, where navvy deaths were recorded. The parish clerk was kept busy, and a note in the company records gives an intimation of just how many entries there were. Twenty pounds was donated towards 'the cost of enlarging the Burial Ground at Chapel le Dale rendered necessary in consequence of the Epidemic small pox among the navvy population'. Smallpox was not the only disease rampant among the shantytowns. Sanitation was all but unknown. The huts were surrounded by cesspools that could only be crossed on rough planks and rats ran everywhere. Diseases such as cholera were rampant and it was not just the men who suffered: the women and children who lived with them shared in the misery. As well as the ravages of disease, there were the all-too-common fatalities, and a memorial tablet was placed in St Leonard's church in Chapel le Dale: 'To the memory of those who through accidents lost their lives in constructing the railway works between Settle and Dent Head. This tablet was erected at the joint expense of their fellow workmen and the railway company 1869 to 1876.'

The largest settlement was at Batty Green and it became a self-contained village with its own slaughterhouse and bakery and was regularly visited by traders from the surrounding districts. A mission hall and a school were built, but there is no record of how many used the facilities. There is, however, a good deal of evidence that local pubs and alehouses were popular and evenings there could get decidedly rough. One night, a navvy drinking at the Gearstones Arms near Ribblehead decided that things were getting a bit tame and decided to liven them up by chucking a stick of dynamite on the fire. It is perhaps not surprising that the pub no longer exists.

Antics such as this only served to provide yet more ammunition for the moralists who were always ready to paint the navvies in the blackest tones.

Their biggest complaints were reserved for those who lived with women they were not formally married to. Rawlinson, who had described the state of the huts on the London & Birmingham Railway, was far more vehement in his condemnation of those who lived there: 'Demoralization existed to a large extent among the female population: the females were corrupted, many of them, and went away with the men, and lived among them in habits that civilised language will scarcely allow a description of.'

There were many myths about the navvies and women. One was about navvy 'weddings'. The ballad *Navvy on the Line* describes how after pay day a navvy went to the pub and sat down next to one of the women:

> I called for a pint of beer, and bid the old wench drink, sir,
> But whilst she was a-drinking, she too at me did wink, sir.
> Well, then we had some talk; in the back we had a rally;
> Then jumped o'er brush and steel, and agreed we'd both live tally.

This was, it was said, the only ceremony needed to declare a man and woman husband and wife – jumping together over a brush and shovel. Whether there is any truth in the story is a different matter. Similarly, the story told at Woodhead about selling a wife for a barrel of beer may be equally dubious. It was roundly denied by the contractor Thomas Nicholson when he gave his evidence to Parliament about the men he employed on the site. His story may not be any prettier, but somehow it seems more likely. And he, more than anyone, was in a position to know:

> Now I dare venture that never such a thing happened on these works as a man selling his wife for a gallon of beer; but I can tell you what happened – I have paid miners and masons from £8 to £16 on a pay; the moment they had got it, they have gone down to the large towns in Yorkshire, Lancashire, and Cheshire, and what do you think they have done with their money? Spent it in the filthy dens of those large towns. Aye, in the back streets among the girls. These men have come back again impregnated with a disease which has cost the club more money than all the sickness besides.

There is no doubt at all that many of the couples that lived together on the line did so without any formal marriage, and some raised families together. Navvies were no different from other men: there were many who looked for the comforts of a family, but saw little point in going to the church which had so often shown indifference to them at best and at worst condemned them out of hand. But whether legally married or living with a navvy, the women often had a very hard life. A young woman from Wiltshire described what it was like when her husband went to look for work on the Leeds & Thirsk Railway:

Well, he was just middling steady, and us was main comfortable for most a year; and then 'twas winter time coming, and they was working nothing but muck. Charley was tipping then, like he is here; and 'tis dreadful hard to get the stuff out of the wagons when 'tis streaming wet atop and all stodge under. Then, you see, he was standing in it over his boots all day long; and once – no, twice – when he draw'd out his foot the sole of his boot was left in the dirt; new ones too, for he had a new pair of 15s boots every week. So he cudn't stand that long. One Saturday night he took out his back money, and said us wld tramp for Yorkshire; for he'd a work'd there and 'twas all rock, and beautiful for tunnels. I didn' know where Yorkshire was, but I hadn' never ben twenty mile nowhere. 'Twas four year agone, and I wasn' but just seventeen year old, and I didn' like for to go; and 'twas then us began for to quarly so. He took his kit, and I had my pillow strapped to my back; and off us set, jawing all along. Us walked thirty mile a day, dead on end; it never stopped raining, and I hadn't a dry thread on me night or day, for us slept in such mis'rable holes of places, I was afeared my clothes 'ud be stole if I took 'em off. But when us comed to Leeds, where Charley know'd a man as kept a public, if I lives a thousand years I shan't never forget the fire and the supper us had that night. But 'tis a filthy, smoky place; and when I seen it by day, I says, Well, if this is Yorkshire, us had better a stopped where us was, dirt and all. And what a lingo they talk! – I cudn' for the life of me understand 'em; and I were glad that Charley cudn' git work he liked there. So us had three days' more tramp – just a hundred mile to a tunnel. They was a rough lot there; and then us seen and done all sorts o' things I wish I'd never heard on.[8]

One can only admire the fortitude of this young woman, tramping huge distances every day in the pouring rain to parts of the country that must have seemed very foreign. There were likely many more who could have told similar stories, just as there were many navvies who worked hard and caused trouble to no one. All they asked was a reasonable pay for work done and fair treatment from those who employed them. Sadly, they could not always rely on receiving either.

CHAPTER TEN

TRUCK, TOMMY AND PAY

Finding accommodation near the worksite was only part of the navvies' problems. They needed food and drink and they certainly expected to have enough money left over from their wages to have the occasional, monumental booze-up. But before they could spend their wages, they had to get them, and that was not always as simple a matter as it should have been.

The system of issuing tokens, as contractors such as Pinkerton had done on the canals, does not seem to have carried over to the railways, but a variation of it did. This was payment by 'truck' or 'tommy note'. At its most basic, a truck system involved paying the men in goods instead of cash. The opportunities for cheating the workforce are all too clear. The employer handed out what he declared was, for example, 5s worth of food to a man, but if the employee had been paid in cash he could have bought the same amount locally for half that amount. It was such an iniquitous system that Parliament passed an Act in 1831 making it illegal in many industries. It did not apply to the railway sites and even if it had, the men would have found, as other workers did, that magistrates simply ignored the law and allowed employers to flaunt it. A very similar system involved issuing tommy notes that could be exchanged for food to a given value, but were only valid in shops owned by the employers. It was difficult for ordinary workmen to get redress. The colliers in Wolverhampton were fortunate in having as a magistrate a local clergyman, the Revd Haden, to take up their cause, but even he had great difficulty in getting men paid in cash, as he explained in a letter to Robert Peel, the Home Secretary.[1] He issued four summonses but was quite unable to get anyone to admit responsibility. 'It was curious to see what artifices they made use of, to prevent my fixing upon the most proper person to pay the just demands of the Complainants. One gave me for an Answer that "he only brings the money to pay the workmen". He then brought forth one Walter Davis (no doubt the Butty Collier) who said that "he was not a Butty Collier, but merely a *Dogger* or overlooker" ... I at last told them that if they did not immediately pay them *in Cash*, I would make an order and enforce it.' He then produced a tommy ticket for 8*s* that could only be used at a shop owned by 'a shopkeeper in league with the Master!' After his first demand produced no reaction, he threatened to take the matter to the High Court, at which point the cash suddenly became available. His actions are notable mainly because they were so out of keeping with the views of other magistrates. Two other parsons who sat on the bench in nearby Bilston declared that they found the local truck system perfectly reasonable – and promised to use the Vagrancy Act against anyone who had the temerity to go around trying to persuade others to rebel against it. This is the background against which the system of payment to navvies has to be seen. Parliament might pass the laws, but local magistrates would seldom act in favour of the men against their employers. In fact, on some occasions, the employers were the magistrates.

It was rare to get redress for workmen, even when there was a sympathetic magistrate who knew the district and the men in it and could see for himself how the truck system was being used to cheat the men. It was even more difficult for the navvies, who appeared in a district as unwelcome strangers, and then tried to persuade local magistrates to use the law on their behalf. On the Richmond Railway at Barnes in November 1845 a ganger called Davis ran his own tommy shop. He took on men and agreed to pay them 2*s* 6*d* a day, but when pay day arrived he handed them notes for his shop. The men went to the magistrate with their notes and said they wanted cash instead. He said as they had already taken the notes he could do nothing, but if they wanted to take the matter further they would have to pay legal fees in advance. It was a classic Catch 22 situation: they had gone to court because they could not get paid in cash, and they could only get payment in cash by paying legal fees with the cash they hadn't got. How could such a situation arise and how could it be allowed to continue?

It is easy to see a sequence of events. Men turned up looking for work and seldom had any cash in hand. So they were advanced money until pay day came round and in the meantime they were given credit. If pay was regular, then the problem was soon solved. But all too often the pay was not regular and the men had to wait a month or more for their money, by which time when they did get cash it all went towards paying off their accumulated debts and they were back where they started. Those who worked the system pointed out that it had its advantages for everyone concerned. The contractors could not pay the men cash up front in case they vanished without doing any work. If they only had a tommy note cashable in a shop owned and run by the contractor or the ganger, then they had no choice but to stay put.

The navvy's life was a hard one – hard work and hard living – and whatever they got they definitely earned.

The other argument was that, in remote locations, it was a way of ensuring that provisions were available at a fair price. Some subcontractors admitted that they often used the system simply to ease their cash problem: they simply didn't have enough money to pay the men. Another argument against using cash was that as payments were regularly made in beer houses it was an open invitation for the navvies to promptly get too drunk to go back to work. One pious gentleman, Thomas Begg of the Scottish Temperance League, seemed to dislike the whole idea of paying anything much at all: 'All my observations of the habit of the working classes, and the influences operating upon them would tell me this, that it is always bad policy to let working men, particularly the lower classes of operative, have large sums of money in their possession at one time.'[2]

There was some justification for the view that paying big sums at once was not a very good idea. Robert Rawlinson, whose evidence was always very clear, was questioned by the Parliamentary Committee:

> Did they lose any time after the pay-day? –Very frequently; in Northamptonshire, after Midsummer, there is a custom there, all the villages have their annual feasts … and so it would go on for three months, and nothing would keep these men from the feasts, and joining in the revelry and drunkenness.

Rawlinson also told the committee that he took care not to go among the men 'if there was drunkenness, or rioting, and they were in crowds; it would not have been safe or judicious to do so'. On the other hand, he said that the men were generally 'amenable to the instructions I had given them' and 'no man ever resisted my authority'.

The whole system of payment was complex. The company paid the contractor, the contractor paid the subcontractor, the subcontractor paid the ganger and the ganger paid the men. Tommy shops could be run by anyone from contractor down to ganger, but it was the ganger who was often the last link between a man and his pay, and he had seldom been chosen for his amicable disposition as evidence to Parliament made clear: 'the ganger merely appears to have been selected from his hardy conduct, and his power to keep men in order. I have in many cases had in evidence the fact that he is a person of very violent character, and not fit to have labourers employed under him.' Often this was the man who would run a beer shop on the line, let the men have credit, and then get them to settle up on pay day. It was, of course, the ganger who kept the accounts. It was a brave navvy who challenged the ganger, and a rare one who had the least idea how much he had drunk during the past weeks. And the gaps between pay days could be very long: at Woodhead it might be as much as nine weeks' wait, and who could remember what he drank nine weeks earlier? Subcontractors also kept ale houses and tommy shops. Peto was one contractor who hated the whole tommy system and would not countenance his own subcontractors using it. He recalled some instances in which those who did use the system made more money from the tommy shop than they did from building the railway. One man made £1,400 profit in four weeks just from his tommy shop.

Peto was not the only influential man who opposed truck and tommy. Sir Charles Wolseley was a principal shareholder in the Trent Valley Railway and he was appalled at what was being done in his name:

> There is shameful work going on on our line of railway, particularly on the score of the Truck System. Now you know as well as I can tell you that cannot be carried on without the aid of those who are subordinate agents – will you then be kind enough to inform me to whom I am to apply to put a stop to it if possible – There has been one strike already and I know from scores of the working men that they are dissatisfied.[3]

Sir Charles's plea made little difference to the way the system operated. The law was of little or no help. If gangers were found to be operating unlawfully, the magistrates' typical response was to threaten to distrain their property, but they were itinerants, living in digs, so they had no property as such. It was an empty threat. Attempts to persuade the company to act were useless; in their view none of this was their responsibility. They paid the contractors; how they in turn paid the men was entirely up to them. On lines up and down the country the abuses continued, and the only time the law intervened was when there was a likelihood of disturbances. Sir Charles had intimated that there had been trouble in the past and would be in the future. But the company's only response was to report on what the contractors proposed to do. They agreed that on one occasion the men had been forced to wait five weeks between pay days and had been 'disorderly'. To prevent further disorder, the obvious course of action was to stop the system that had created the problem in the first place; instead, they allowed the system to continue and brought in the police to keep control of the men. The only concession made by the contractors was to promise to pay up at four-weekly intervals, and to allow the navvies money on account. That sounds reasonable enough, but the company also noted that the money could only be spent in the subcontractors' tommy shop, where goods were, in the company's own statement, 'charged from twenty to fifty per cent more for most articles, than they would be at a common shop'. In other words, the abuses would continue but anyone daring to complain too vigorously would have to do so under the eye of the local police. Most magistrates made their position quite clear: it was not their job to arbitrate between employers and men, just keep the peace.

It would have seemed to be in the company's own interest to control the system. If the navvies could not get the protection of the law, there was bound to be trouble and if there was trouble then it disrupted the work. Many

companies produced legal documents, which they required contractors and
subcontractors to sign, agreeing that they would neither operate tommy shops
nor sell beer. But when the agreements were flaunted, the companies were as
reluctant as the magistrates to step in; what went on between employers and
men was no one else's business. In some ways one can sympathise with the
subcontractors. Like the navvies, they often suffered from delayed payments
from further up the pecking order, and one way to keep going was to run a
'Tom-and-Jerry' as the beer shops were known.

Looking through the records, although there are many accounts of 'disturbances' over pay and even full-blown riots, there appear to have been far fewer
strikes. This is not, perhaps, too surprising. A gang of men with a grievance,
meeting in pubs, could feed on each other's anger until the whole situation
exploded into violence. It needed no organisation, no co-ordinator. The way
in which the navvies were organised in small gangs made it far more difficult
to put together a coherent plan for strike action and even when a strike did go
ahead, there was always the possibility of the men simply being dismissed, as
had happened at the Severn Tunnel. Itinerant navvies were constantly looking
for work, and even those who went on strike were liable to get fed up with
having neither work nor pay. They were as likely to pack up their belongings
and head for another line as they were to stand firm. Given the situation, it is
not surprising that strikes were rare and seldom successful. Two examples are
typical of what happened to striking navvies:

> On Friday the whole workers of the Scottish Central lines from Peterhead to
> Thornhill amounting upwards of 3000 sturdy labourers armed with shovels
> assembled in front of the offices at Stirling when they demanded an advance of
> wages of 3s per week. The manager of the works considering the shortness of
> the day the rate of wages at present being 2s 6d per day did not think it proper
> to comply with what seemed to be an unreasonable demand; and as it was feared
> some disturbance might take place every precautionary measure was adopted
> and the workmen are now regretting their rash step and are resolved to return to
> their work. Some of the ring leaders have been paid off.[4]

It is probable that the ringleaders were merely the spokesmen who had been
persuaded to argue the case for the others. The strike had fizzled out: they
were the obvious scapegoats and they paid the penalty. It did not encourage
others to take the lead in any strike action.

On the Scottish line there were simply too many involved to sack the lot,
but another strike at much the same time at the opposite end of the country
was treated very differently:

> The labourers on the Richmond railway 700 in number have struck for an
> advance in their wages of 6d a day. The contractor refuses to give it: declared that

he will not again employ one of the strikers, and has advertised for other hands promising 3s 6d and 4s a-day and no tommy-shops.[5]

It is interesting to note that both these strikes in 1846 were for an extra 6d a day, but even if the navvies in Scotland had got the raise, it would only have brought them up to 3s a day, still less than the rate being advertised by the Richmond contractor. It was the awareness of this sort of situation that sent navvies off on the tramp. There was a navvy grapevine, which passed on news of likely jobs around the country. If a navvy turned up on site, even if a job wasn't available, the other navvies would give him a good meal and tell him the latest news about where men were being hired.

No one ever described navvies as steady characters. Unlike other workers who might be tied to a factory or mine, they were free to roam when the mood took them. They were also liable to take time off given the right circumstances. Pay day provided one of those circumstances. These were not thrifty men, and having money in their pockets they liked to spend it, preferably on beer, or stronger spirits if they happened to be available. It became known as going on the randy. One of the disadvantages of having long gaps between pay days was that when they did come round the men had quite a lot of money to spend – and they could take a few days to spend it, and a few more to recover from the effects. The employers described them as squandering their money on 'every sort of lewdness and bad women'. They were often portrayed as almost a subhuman species. 'Like dogs released from a week's confinement, they ran about and did not know what to do with themselves … Their presence spread like a plague.'[6]

There have been quite enough descriptions of navvy riots to get the general picture that things could, and did, go wrong when randies got out of hand, but some people tried a different approach to locking the navvies up or sacking them. They wanted to reform them.

There were many attempts to persuade the clergy to preach to the navvies. There were even good suggestions of what sort of man would be suitable for the job. 'A Clergyman – energetic – zealous – and judicious. A gentleman easy of address, free of access, possessed of skill and tact – and withal a plain and earnest speaker, and devoted to his work.'[7] There were men who met that exacting standard, who went among the navvies and treated them as fellow human beings not animals. Many of the traditional clergy, however, found it difficult to connect. University educated, from privileged backgrounds, they belonged to a very different world from that of the rough navvies. The evangelical, nonconformist preachers often found it easier to talk to the men. William Breakey of the Town Missionary Society went to the Chester & Holyhead Railway, where many of the workers were Welsh, taking with him Bibles, printed in Welsh on one page and English on the facing page. He sold 374 of them. One of the most successful preachers was Peter Thompson, known as Happy Peter, who spoke the language of the navvies because he had himself been a navvy.

Some contractors personally encouraged the movement. Peto was among them, urged on by his very zealous Baptist wife. He handed out improving tracts and Bibles, though with the latter he made sure they would really be read and not sold to buy beer. He also paid lay preachers out of his own pocket. All this was on a very ad hoc basis and it was not until the 1870s that there was any coherent, organised attempt to bring religion, and sobriety, to the navvy world.

Elizabeth Garrett Anderson is best known as Britain's first official woman doctor and for her pioneering work in getting other qualified women accepted by the rest of the medical profession; but she was also involved in a number of different charities. She was present at the ceremony to unveil the navvy monument in Otley churchyard and this was her inspiration to take an active interest in the welfare of the railway workers. Later she was to meet a Leeds vicar, Lewis Moule, who founded the Navvy Mission Society. Encouraged by his work, she helped to found the Christian Excavators' Union. It was hardly a huge success, never having a membership of more than 300, but it did provide real benefits. They set up soup kitchens when times were hard and also simple reading rooms, where navvies who were literate read out news items to the rest. Some of the reading matter consisted of the ordinary newspapers of the day, but there was never a shortage of improving, evangelical tracts. A popular theme was the evil of alcohol and the virtue of abstinence. Some of the broadsheet ballads that describe some of the more raucous aspects of navvy life have already been quoted, and somehow they seem to provide rather more credible portraits of the average navvy than this pious song:

> Yes, I am an English navvy: but, oh, not an English sot.
> I have run my pick through alcohol, in bottle, glass, or pot;
> And with the spade of abstinence, and all the power I can,
> I am spreading out a better road for every working man.

It is easy to make fun of such a naive song, but missions such as the Excavators' Union gave real practical help to a band of men who so many others either vilified or simply ignored altogether. Life cannot have been easy for the lay preachers and it would have been easy to become discouraged by the lack of response and attitude of indifference of many they tried to preach to and help.

Throughout the period of both canal and railway construction – a time covering well over a hundred years – for every one who praised the navvy there were a dozen to condemn him. Not many who used the canals and railways and blessed them as wonders of modern transport gave much thought to the men who built them. Even when they were actually at work at a construction site it was seldom that anyone knew what they were really called. And when the work was finished and the men marched away, people spoke of the line as having been built by Stephenson or Brunel and nobody remembered Scandalous or the Horse Shoe Gang. But just once in the whole history of the navvies, the men emerged not as villains but as the heroes of the hour.

CHAPTER ELEVEN

THE NATION'S HEROES

The Crimean War is mostly remembered for monumental failures rather than famous victories. Tennyson immortalised the Charge of the Light Brigade and made it appear as a glorious example of the bravery of the British soldiers, which it certainly was, though even then he had to add one essential proviso:

> 'Forward the Light Brigade!'
> Was there a man dismay'd
> Not tho' the soldiers knew
> Some one had blunder'd.

Indeed they had blundered, 'they' being the generals who sent the men to certain death. The other great scandal was exposed by William Howard Russell of *The Times* who reported on the atrocious conditions and inadequate nursing at the four military hospitals at Scutari, and forced the government to take action. It was only later that the full scale of the horror was revealed. Although 4,000 men died of wounds received in the fighting, 17,000 were killed by the diseases rampant in the places supposed to be curing sickness not creating it. Famously, one woman went to Scutari, where she set about imposing discipline and new standards of hygiene. Her name was Florence Nightingale. But there is one other story that should be better known, and that is the story of the British navvies. To understand the story and why the navvies were needed, you need to appreciate something about the war itself and how it was run.

The political background is comparatively straightforward. Russia was gaining strength as a world power and was anxious to extend its influence. Turkey lay at the heart of the rapidly decaying Ottoman Empire. Relations between the two powers might have seemed of little importance to the countries of Western Europe, but between them lay the Black Sea, and whoever controlled that held a strategic position from which they could control the land routes to Asia. Russia had that prize in view and was looking for a pretext to declare war on Turkey. It found a variety of strange excuses for the conflict, including an argument over who had the right to hold the keys to the Holy Sepulchre in Bethlehem. In November 1853 the Russian Fleet attacked the far inferior Turkish navy and annihilated it. Some 3,000 Turkish sailors died.

Britain had no intention of allowing the Russians to gain absolute control over the region, and the press whipped up a frenzy of indignation against the monstrous Russian bear. The strategic key to the whole area was the Crimean peninsula that thrust out from the northern coast of the Black Sea. In March 1854 Britain and France declared war on Russia, and the British Army set sail for the Crimea.

The army had not been involved in any conflicts since the end of the Napoleonic Wars and was run by ageing generals and aristocratic officers who put parade ground drill ahead of military tactics. Regiments vied with each other over the splendour of their uniforms, which became ever more extravagant: the ordinary soldier could be forgiven for his inability to fire a musket with any degree of accuracy, but not for having a dirty button. The officers who were in command were not there on merit: they had purchased their commissions. Lord Palmerston declared that the system was essential 'to connect the higher classes of Society with the Army; and he did not know any more effective method of connecting them than by allowing members of high family who held commissions to get on with more rapidity than they would by seniority'.[1] The alternative was to have the army commanded by 'unprincipled military adventurers'; in other words, professional soldiers. The result was witnessed in the Crimea: one young Hussar officer arrived with two carriages, one of which carried his plate and linen, a stud of fine horses and three grooms. On being told that he was to be posted away from base and would have to leave his retinue behind, he simply announced that a gentleman could not be expected to do anything so outrageous, packed up and went home. Meanwhile, one whole Guards regiment was so weakened by disease, poor rations and wretched equipment that they could not march more than 5 miles a day, and they could only manage that if their packs were carried on carts. It is against this background that one has to view the events that developed as the British Army laid siege to the Russian fortress of Sevastopol (also referred to as Sebastopol).

The army had enjoyed some early successes but had never followed them through – Lord Lucan famously refused to engage the enemy on one occasion when there had been a real chance of a victory and earned himself the nickname 'Lord Look-on'. Now the army was encamped on the muddy plain round Sevastopol and faced new enemies: hunger and disease rather than the Russians. A major problem was communications: fetching up stores from the ships in the harbour at Balaclava. Unfortunately, the campaign had started in September, when freezing winds and driving rain turned the ground into a quagmire. Thirty thousand men, living in tents, had nothing to connect them to the outside world except a totally inadequate dirt road. Henry Clifford, one of the officers, described the situation in a letter home:

> Our next affliction is want of transport for the Army. It is too bad that Government has made no provision in this department. We have, till lately, been entirely dependent upon the Russian ox wagons captured when first we landed and a few Turkish ponies with pack saddles to bring our rations and forage for horses from Balaclava, a distance of about four or five miles. But the cold, want of food, and hard work have killed the oxen and ponies, and the roads are impassable. We now only get a quarter and a half of rations of pork and biscuits, which is brought up by the few remaining ponies, and we are obliged to send out Chargers to Balaclava for their forage.[2]

The situation was dire and getting worse. Conscientious military leaders, such as Sir John Burgoyne, tried to stir the authorities into action. He told a sorry story of not being able to get essential supplies to feed the troops and how that in turn prevented them working efficiently. It became increasingly difficult to move guns and shells to where they were needed. The men were so exhausted that two sentries fell asleep at their posts and were bayoneted by a Russian raiding party. He did not blame the men themselves, but he realised that such events threatened the security of the whole camp, He appealed to Lord Raglan, the commander of the expeditionary force: 'The army is sickly to a grievous extent, and is declining numerically as well as physically.'

In spite of the obvious grave difficulties, it is doubtful that anything would have been done if the public in Britain had not been made aware of the dire situation. Once again, it was Russell, *The Times* correspondent, who was mainly responsible. He was admirably terse and clearly both angry and frustrated at what he found: 'there is nothing to eat, nothing to drink, no roads, no communications; the only thing in abundance is cholera.' Parliament was forced to act and the Duke of Newcastle led the campaign to do something about the situation. One member had a very practical proposal. Morton Peto was now a MP, and he suggested that they build a railway to link the port at Balaclava with the camp at Sevastopol. In December, the Duke was able to write that Peto, together with his business partner Betts, had offered to build the railway 'with no other condition than that they shall reap no pecuniary advantage from it'. Peto now called on Brassey to lend his support and together the two most powerful railway contractors in the world set about organising the whole scheme. The Duke was not quite accurate in stating that the contractors had made 'no other condition'. They had, in fact, made one very important stipulation. If they took their navvy army to the Crimea it would be answerable only to them. They would not take orders from officers, nor would they be subject to army discipline. Given the reports coming back from the war zone, they had very little reason to place any trust in the army's organisational abilities.

The first thing the two contractors did was to contact railway companies all over Britain to persuade them to provide the essential supplies for the enterprise. It would have been hard to resist two such powerful men, who carried the full weight of public support behind them. Peto took it upon himself to start the process by sending one of his principal agents, Beattie, with a full engineering staff to survey a possible route. Their arrival was greeted with huge enthusiasm in the Crimea, and one of the officers, Colonel Gordon, who was encamped at Sevastopol, wrote that in his view the railway was the only salvation for the beleaguered forces: 'Without the railroad I do not see how we can bring up guns and ammunition in sufficient quantities to silence the guns of the enemy.'

All that was needed now was for the men to build the line. Offices were opened in Waterloo Road, London, and as word spread the navvies crowded in to sign up. There was a very real incentive: the men were being offered a six-month contract at a high rate of pay: 5 to 8s a day. Many might well have been swept along by the popular, patriotic fervour, and that was certainly the view the popular press took. The papers that had scarcely bothered to mention the navvies at all unless they were striking or rioting now took a very different approach, praising them as the heroes of the hour. This was an article in the *Illustrated London News*:

> The men employed in our engineering works have been long known as the very élite of England, as to physical power; broad, muscular, massive fellows who are scarcely to be matched in Europe. Animated, too, by as ardent a British spirit as beats under any uniform, if ever these men come to hand-to-hand fighting with the enemy, they will fell them like ninepins. Disciplined and enough of them, they could walk from end to end of the continent.

The contractors had no intention of getting their navvies into any fighting at all with the enemy, but that did not stop the popular press fantasising. A *Punch* cartoon showed the navvies, armed only with shovels and pickaxes, laying into the Russian troops, who collapsed under the onslaught. There were also sarcastic comments contrasting the practical abilities of the sturdy navvy with the effete officer class who were making such a mess of the campaign. Another cartoon in *Punch* had two navvies looking at a top-hatted gent and one saying to the other: 'Ah, Bill! It shows the forrard march of the age. First the brute force, such as 'im, and then the likes of us to do it scientific, and show the might of intellect.' Seldom has public opinion undergone such a complete volte-face.

Brassey described his part in the operation with pride, as he had every right to do, for it was a masterly operation, carried out with great efficiency: 'We succeeded in sending out twenty-five large steamers with men, horses, railway engines, commissariat and other stores, in a very short time.' He made it sound very straightforward, but in reality it was far from being that simple. Peto's part-ner, Edward Betts, who had the job of organising the transport, wrote: 'from the great difficulty of obtaining ships we have been obliged to pay higher rates for chartering and have been compelled to buy three screw steamers and a sailing ship instead of hiring.'[3] Peto himself, who had now branched out from civil engineering and was running the North European Steam Navigation Company, was forced to send his own ships to help out: not every shipping magnate wanted his valuable vessels sent to a war zone. Altogether, 500 men set off in the ships, of whom 300 were navvies, 100 carpenters, 30 masons, 30 blacksmiths, 12 engine drivers and a few specialist tradesmen. There were also three doctors and, more surprisingly, three scripture readers. Each navvy was fully equipped to a standard that must have been the envy of the demoral-ised soldiers now straggling back to Britain, wounded or ravaged with disease. Each man had the following items:

1 painted bag
1 painted suit
2 coloured cotton shirts
1 flannel shirt (red)
1 flannel shirt (white)
1 flannel belt
1 pr Moleskin trousers
1 moleskin vest lined with serge
1 fear nought slop [this strangely named garment was a heavy woollen jacket]
1 pr long water-proof boots
1 pr Fishermen boots
1 blue cravat
1 blue worsted cravat
1 pr Leggings
1 pr Boots
1 strap and buckle
1 bed and pillow
1 pr Mittens
1 rug and blanket
1 pr of blankets
1 woollen coat
1 pr grey stockings
2 lb tobacco

Some of the men, it was said, had added guns to the luggage, rather hoping for a chance to have a go at the Russians themselves, even if they were supposed to have nothing to do with any military operation.

Given the charge of immorality and irresponsibility so often laid against the navvies, it is worth noting that their departure from London was held up by them queuing to sign papers that allowed the contractors to make payments to their families while they were away. When they were ready to embark, the Duke of Newcastle, who had continued to take a keen and active interest in the whole affair, arrived with Peto to see them off. The Duke asked why there was such a large pile of tarpaulins waiting to be loaded. He was told they were to be used as temporary shelters for the navvies until more permanent wooden huts were available. This impressed the Duke, who commented: 'What a good thing if some could be sent out to our poor soldiers, who have to sleep on the bare ground!' Peto said there was no reason why they couldn't be, and he could get as many as were needed in a matter of days. Delighted, the Duke returned to London and passed on the good news to the Ordnance Department. The department that had signally failed to supply any such comforts itself promptly turned the proposal down, expressing astonishment and horror at such blatantly 'irregular' proceedings.

The ships set sail with their consignment of men, equipment, sleepers and rails. They were delayed by stormy seas in the Bay of Biscay, but finally made it as far as Gibraltar, where the navvies were allowed to go ashore and where they promptly got riotously drunk. There was a second stop at Malta, where they did it all over again. At the last stop before the war zone, Constantinople, the authorities decided, probably wisely, that this time the navvies had better stay on board. By the time they reached the Crimea, seasickness had been forgotten and they were in a good mood and ready for work. Some soldiers were delighted to see them, and one officer described them as 'fine, manly fellows'. Others were not so sure, and were equally dubious about the value of having a railway at all. Captain Clifford, who had complained about the poor transport earlier, was one of those critics. On 8 February 1855, he wrote: 'The navvies look "unutterable things" at Balaclava, but have set to work at "The Railway" more because it is their nature to do so than anything else. For my part, I wish they would make us a good road, for I have little faith in the proposed Railway.'[4]

Four days later he had completely changed his mind:

I am astonished to see the progress of The Railway at Balaclava on Friday. The Navvies in spite of the absence of beefsteaks and 'Barkley & Perkins Entire' [beer] work famously, and as I have before mentioned do more work in a day, than a Regiment of English Soldiers can do in a week.

The army was now camped out on a ridge, 12 miles from Balaclava. Brassey's instructions to his agent Beattie were succinct: 'You will, in laying your road, be not over-particular about levels; repair and make it more perfect after, for the promptitude with which you can supply the army with this road will be its chief recommendation.' In any case it was not expected to last, as everyone hoped the campaign would soon be over. Sir John Burgoyne, who as Colonel-Commandant of the Royal Engineers should have known what he was talking about, was enthusiastic about the work. He wrote on 11 February from Balaclava:

> I am happy to say the railway works are progressing. They have a line of rails from the centre of the town to a little way out; from about half a mile further they will have a very steep incline, and a stationary engine, and, when workable to the top of the heights, will be of vast service.

The speed and effort put in was quite extraordinary. One of the first tasks facing the men was the bridging of a stream. In the afternoon that work was to start, a pile driver was delivered to the site in pieces. It was erected, piles were driven, the bridge constructed and the tracks advanced another 100 yards, all within twenty-four hours. Within ten days of work starting the tracks had reached the village of Kadikoi, and although locomotives were not in use, ammunition could be loaded on to trucks instead of being passed from hand to hand by lines of men. The top of the escarpment, 4½ miles from the coast, was reached by 31 March, and this made a huge difference to the supply routes. The men were laying a double track of rails, with the centre planked over so that it could be used by horses. Eventually, a complex railway system was in operation, which included a branch line to the Ordnance depot. By the time the navvies left, 39 miles of track had been laid.

Almost everyone was praising the navvies for their endeavours. A few sour notes were struck by Russell of *The Times*. One of his reports concentrated on fighting that had broken out on one of the hulks in the harbour where some of the men were lodged. He argued that it could all have been sorted out very quickly if only the military police had been allowed to intervene; but the navvies had been specifically excluded from military control. Russell described the affair as almost leading to a full-scale riot. But even he had to admit they were prodigious workers, and he was soon given an example of just how fast work was proceeding. He had gone off for a day to the camp at Sevastopol, leaving behind the comfortable house where he was staying, surrounded by a walled garden. By the time he returned, there were tracks where the walls had been. He was staring at the transformation when there was an almighty crash and the whole house shook. He went to investigate and found that over-enthusiastic workers had felled a tree, which had fallen on the house, damaging the roof and carrying away a balcony. One does wonder whether or not someone had happened to mention that Mr Russell was being critical of the navvies.

The Severn Tunnel, finally opened to traffic on 1 December 1886, had been an immense work, which at its busiest had employed over 3,000 men.

News of the success reached London and the press was full of praise for the men who had made it possible:

> It ought to be consolatory to Mr. Carlyle and the mourners over the degeneracy of these latter-days, that there is at least one institution, and that a pre-eminently English one, which, despite climatic drawbacks and all sorts of deteriorating influences, exhibits all its original stamina and pristine healthiness. Everything we hear and read, from every quarter, testifies to the energetic, skilled, and matured progression of the great undertaking now progressing between Balaclava and the cannon-bristling heights of Sevastopol, and there cannot be a doubt that, when it has reached its terminus, those engaged upon it may safely adopt the motto of their honoured chief, Sir Morton Peto – *Ad Finem Fidelis* [faithful to the end].[5]

Once the railway was completed, the army would have liked the navvies to stay on to help construct fortifications, but their work was done. It was now up to the army to make use of their great achievement. The army responded by instantly imposing restrictions. The Commissariat decreed that no supplies should be sent before 8.00 in the morning or after 5.30 in the afternoon. Navvies might be expected to work all day and night, but that was not what the army expected of its men, and certainly not the officers who would have had to supervise the operation. Nevertheless, the construction of the railway did its job. The army was fed, the guns supplied with ammunition and in September 1855 British soldiers marched into Sevastopol.

In order to work using government funds, Peto had to resign his seat in Parliament, but he was rewarded with a baronetcy. Beattie, who had worked harder than anyone in controlling the whole operation in the Crimea, was less fortunate. He was injured in an accident on the line, came home and overcome by his injury and exhaustion he died. The navvies also came home, collected their pay and set off to look for work.

There was one other gang of workmen who were to go to the Crimea. In the winter of 1854/55 there were 12,500 British troops in the notorious hospital at Scutari. Florence Nightingale had railed against the bureaucracy that did nothing, while the wounded died from infection and disease, and her wrath was concentrated on the Permanent Undersecretary at the War Office, Sir Benjamin Hawes – 'a dictator, an autocrat'. But Hawes knew exactly who to go to for help: his brother-in-law just happened to be Britain's most famous railway engineer, Isambard Kingdom Brunel. He wrote to him asking if he could possibly design a prefabricated hospital to send out to the Crimea. Brunel responded immediately with enthusiasm that if he could be of help then he would use 'my best exertions without any limitations' to get the job done. He was as good as his word: within six days Hawes had the proposals and plans on his desk.

He based his design on standard units that could easily be assembled on site and then joined together to form the complete hospital. The basic wooden buildings that formed the standard units consisted of two wards, each holding twenty-four beds, a room for the nurses, water closets and outhouses. The units were to be joined together by covered passageways. Each patient was to be allowed plenty of space and the buildings were kept ventilated by fans. Cleanliness was ensured by providing washbasins, a bath for the patients and a built-in wooden trunk for drainage. Metal was used for the kitchen, bakery and laundry as a fire precaution. Altogether, there was provision for 1,000 patients.

In April 1855, just two months after Brunel had been given the request, the hospitals were packed up ready for shipment and Brunel sent his workmen and a doctor to supervise the work. One of Brunel's assistants, John Brunton, was sent on ahead and he received detailed instructions from Brunel:

> By steamer *Hawk* or *Gertrude* I shall send you a derrick and most of the tools, and as each vessel sails you shall hear by post what is in her. You are most fortunate in having exactly the man in Dr. Parkes that I should have selected – an enthusiastic, clever agreeable man, devoted to the object, understanding the plans and works and quite disposed to attach as much importance to the perfection of the building and all other parts I deem most important as to mere doctoring.
>
> The son of the contractor goes with the head foreman, ten carpenters, the foreman of the WC makers and two men who worked on the iron houses and can lay pipes. I am sending a small forge and two carpenters' benches, but you will need assistant carpenters and labourers, fifty to sixty in all.[6]

Brunel had little or no faith in the competence of the military, so he added a rider, heavily underlined: 'I shall have sent you excellent assistants – try and succeed. Do not let <u>anything induce you to alter the general system and arrangements that I have laid down</u>.' His lack of confidence in the army proved well founded. They declined to offer any help, so the gang who had arrived from England simply got on with it and did everything themselves, following Brunel's detailed instructions, which even included notes on where to put the boxes for toilet paper. The first patients moved in just seven weeks after work started. In comparison with the horrendous death rate at Scutari, the Brunel hospitals were a tremendous success: of the 1,500 who were treated there, only twenty-five died. Hundreds, possibly thousands of British soldiers owed their lives to the railway engineer and his tiny workforce.

It was claimed that more Union Pacific navvies were murdered in the camps than died in accidents.

For the navvies and the tradesmen who went to the Crimea, it represented no more than an interlude in their lives, though it was a glorious one. Once back in Britain they returned to their normal work. But the Crimea was certainly not the only place outside the British Isles where railways were being constructed. British engineers and contractors were in demand all over the world, and often they took the British navvies with them.

CHAPTER TWELVE

THE NAVVY OVERSEAS

D uring the canal age, there was no great demand for British expertise from other countries. In Europe, the Low Countries had been
constructing canals for centuries; France's magnificent Canal du
Midi had been completed almost a century before the Duke of Bridgewater
had even begun his canal. The one exception was Sweden, where Count Von
Platen, in 1810, was the driving force behind the plan for a ship canal to cut
right across the country, linking the North Sea to the Baltic. It was to make
use of the navigable River Gota for part of the route, and would then consist
of wholly artificial waterways to link a series of natural lakes. In many ways it
was similar to the Caledonian Canal, which linked a number of lochs in its
passage across Scotland, and Von Platen persuaded Thomas Telford to be con-
sulting engineer for what was to become the Gotha Canal. Von Platen had no
shortage of labourers: he was able to draw on the resources of the army, who
provided him with 900 soldiers as well as 150 Russian prisoners of war. But he
was still concerned about how unfamiliar the men were with canal work. The
Norwegian resident engineer Samuel Bagge wrote to Telford to ask for help:

> I most earnestly wish you did succeed in your kind promise to send me some
> tools and some experienced workmen, especially people accustomed to the
> puddling process, as it is very little known, and I dare say, there is nobody here
> ever has seen it practiced, except for myself and it was only for a short time I did
> see it. Could you also procure us some workmen for the masonry work, it would
> be of unaccountable service, as we are for the most part destitute of such people
> familiar to your mode of building locks.[1]

No doubt volunteers could have been found to go to Sweden for a suitable
reward, but this was 1810 and Britain was at war with France. It was one thing
to risk injury in building a canal, but quite another to face the danger of
being blown to smithereens by an enemy ship – even if a ship could be found

willing to make the passage. In the event, the best Telford could do was to send a few key men to oversee the work and train up the locals. He also sent some 'working utensils', which would make the workers more efficient – the canal works would, he said, be Sweden's 'Canal Academy'. In the event, it all worked out very well. James Simpson, one of Telford's trusted assistants, reported that the Swedish workmen were 'very willing' to be taught, and when he went to inspect a finished lock, he declared the work to be excellent, 'although none of them had ever had a pick or a hammer into their hands before 12 months last Spring'.[2] The canal was opened in 1829 and marked the end of British involvement in European canal construction.

Railway construction presented a very different picture, since Britain was well ahead of the rest of the world and was setting an example that many others wanted to follow. It was here that the first steam locomotives had run over rails, where the first public railway had been built and the first intercity line to be run by steam locomotives was opened. One of the first countries to show an interest was not, as might have been expected, one of the industrially advanced nations of Western Europe, but Russia. Grand Duke Nicholas was an enthusiast for modern technology and made a point of visiting Britain, where he went to see the pioneering Middleton Colliery Railway. Later, as Tsar Nicholas I, he authorised a line to be constructed from St Petersburg to the Imperial Summer Palace at Tsarokoe Selo. The rails were sent from Merthyr Tydfil and four locomotives were ordered from Britain, one of which was designed by Timothy Hackworth, based at the Shildon works on the Stockton & Darlington Railway. Hackworth's son John was sent with a foreman and a small team of erectors to put the machine together and initiate the Russians in the mysteries of steam locomotion. For a young man who had never left England before, it turned out to be quite an adventure. St Petersburg harbour was closed by ice, so they had to disembark at the nearest Baltic port and travel the rest of the way by sleigh. Young Hackworth nonchalantly described the cold, which even froze the whisky in their flasks, and how they were pursued across the snow by a pack of wolves.[3] The early experiments with the locomotives were not entirely successful. The first British engines had been required by law to 'consume their own smoke', which in practice meant using coke as fuel. In Russia they hurled logs into the firebox, sending a shower of sparks up the chimney which, carried by the wind, set fire to the clothes of passengers travelling behind the engine in an open coach. When a cylinder cracked in the cold, George Thompson, the foreman who had travelled with Hackworth, had a pattern made and set off on the 600-mile journey to Moscow, where he had a new cylinder cast. Life in the early days of the Russian railways was certainly not boring.

Russia made use of British expertise but not British muscle. Things went very differently in France. Here, too, the first reaction was to call in British engineering experts to help with the planning. Charles Vignoles conducted the first survey in 1833 for a line from Paris that would go through the Channel ports to provide a rail link to London. The finance was never forthcoming, but instead a new proposal was put forward. On the English side of the Channel, there would be a route from London to Southampton, the cost of which would be partly paid by the French government. On the French side, the line would run from Paris to Dieppe, with a branch line to Rouen. The English engineer Joseph Locke was to be in charge of the whole operation. At first he intended to let the work to French contractors, but when their bids came in they were far too high, so tenders were put out in Britain. Two of the leading men, Thomas Brassey and William Mackenzie, put in bids and agreed to share the work. A familiar story was repeated. The Normandy locals did not appear to be physically capable of building the lines, so the contractors set about recruiting British navvies for the job. Locke described what happened when Brassey and Mackenzie arrived in France:

> Among the appliances carried by these gentlemen, there were none more striking or important than the navvies themselves. Following in the wake of their masters, when it was known that they had contracted for works in France, the men soon spread over Normandy, where they became objects of interest to the community, not only by the peculiarity of their dress, but by their uncouth size, habits, and manners; which formed so marked a contrast with those of the peasantry of that country. These men were generally employed in the most difficult and laborious work, and by that means earned larger wages than the rest of the men. Discarding the wooden shovels and basket-sized barrows of the Frenchmen, they used the tools which modern art had suggested, and which none but the most expert and robust could wield.[4]

Brassey had one advantage over other contractors, in that his wife who joined him spoke fluent French. Edward Mackenzie, the younger brother of the contractor William, found his ignorance of the language a handicap on many occasions. A typical diary entry reads: 'I measured the Gangers who were finished at the side cuttings & could not pay them, Smith the Interpreter not having met me to appointment.'[5] Clearly, although the British contractors took navvies with them to France, they also relied heavily on local labourers. It is difficult to estimate exactly how the workforce was constituted. Evidence to the 1846 Parliamentary Committee stated that there were 10,000 British on the Paris and Rouen line, but the directors of the railway in their report to shareholders claimed that the French were in the majority, working with 'the comparatively small number of Englishmen, whom the contractors have felt it necessary to send over to France, in order to show how works of this sort are conducted'. The French railway magazine *Journal des Chemin de fer* reported that of the 12,000 men working on the line in November 1841, 2,000 were British. Allowing for a certain patriotic inflation of numbers, it would seem that the French journal's estimate of 2,000 British navvies could be taken as a minimum and that there were probably never more than 5,000.[6] The rest of the workforce was made up of the French themselves, and a smattering of workers from other European countries. As well as employing a multinational workforce, the contractors had to sign contracts that complied with French laws. There was one striking difference between these contracts and those signed back in Britain. As we have seen, the company and contractors rarely took responsibility for problems that directly affected the navvies, particularly when it came to accidents. Things in France were very different, and the following clauses from the Amiens & Boulogne Railway are typical:

> The Contractor to remain civilly responsible of the acts of his men and agents, as well as of all accidents that may arise on the works.
>
> The prices of the undertaking are established on a scale sufficiently large for help and relief to be given to men or to their families on account of accidents.
>
> All expenses incurred for help or relief to men on account of accidents … to be deducted from the sum due to the Contractor.

There was also a clause specifically forbidding the use of any kind of truck system or payment in anything other than legal currency.

The directors' report spoke of the British navvies being mainly employed to show the locals how things were to be done, which must have been quite interesting given the total lack of understanding of each other's language. One of Brassey's agents noted that there were eleven languages spoken on the Paris and Rouen line, including one solitary Portuguese speaker, who struggled along with a little French. Even among the British, the different groups used four languages between themselves – English, Welsh, Irish and Scots Gaelic. But somehow orders were given and understood. 'They pointed to the earth to be moved, or the wagon to be filled, said the word "d–n" emphatically, stamped their feet, and somehow or other instructions, thus conveyed, were generally comprehended by the foreigner.'[7] Supervisors, such as Edward Mackenzie, could rely on their interpreters, but in time the motley workforce managed to sort its own way of doing things:

> But among the navvies there grew up a language which could hardly be said to be either French or English; and which in fact, must have resembled that strange compound pigeon English [sic] which is spoken at Hong Kong by the Chinese … This composite language had its own forms and grammar; and it seems to have been made use of in other countries besides France; for afterwards there were young Savoyards who became quite skilled in the use of this particular language, and who were employed as cheap interpreters between the sub-contractors and the native workmen.[8]

Surprisingly, given the English reputation as bad linguists, the navvies picked up French quite quickly. Brassey's agent noted wryly that they 'did eventually acquire a considerable knowledge of French, not, of course, speaking it very grammatically, but still having a greater knowledge and command of it, than they had their native tongue'. Apart from language differences, there were also different attitudes towards living accommodation at the works. Unlike the British navvies working at home, they seem to have had no difficulties finding lodgings with the locals in the many villages strung out along the route. The German workers, by contrast, were apparently happy to take anything offered: 'They would put up with a barn or anything.'

Arthur Helps's biography of Brassey contains a surprisingly large amount of detail on the lives of the navvies in France. The horror stories of riotous drunkenness were not repeated. There was a certain amount of trouble at first, simply because the navvies discovered that brandy was remarkably cheap – and drank it at about the same rate as the French drank wine:

> But after a short time the French found they were a good natured sort of people, who spent their money freely. Hence they were always kindly received; and even the gendarmes themselves began very soon to see which was the best way of managing the Englishmen. They got sometime unruly on pay-day, but not as a rule.

Their good conduct may be partly due to the fact that contractors such as Brassey and Mackenzie were able to take their pick of the best men. Like the navvies who went to war in the Crimea, these men showed a sense of responsibility. They did not bring wives and families to France, but they sent money home on a regular basis, and even the unmarried men regularly sent money to their parents. It was reported that quite a lot of the single men married French women, but whether it was a 'navvy wedding' or one that would be officially recognised by the French authorities is not mentioned. In many ways the men acclimatised themselves well and fitted in with local customs, but not in everything. One of Brassey's officials noted that the navvy, 'like most of his countrymen, of whatever rank or occupation, scorned the habits or the dress of the people he lived amongst'. He wore the same 'uniform' that was worn by the navvies at home, and when he couldn't find the traditional high-laced boots to buy, he paid to have them made.

From the first, there were discrepancies in pay between the British navvies and the rest. This reflected the amount of work that each group could do. The experienced navvies could shift twice as much as the locals in a day, and as a consequence, they got four and a half francs a day as opposed to two francs for the French. At first the French workers were delighted as that was far more than they had ever earned before, and they described the contractors as 'angels from heaven'. But as time went on, and they became hardened and accustomed to the work, their wages rose to four francs. Gradually, the demand for British labourers diminished, and as more railways were built, so the French took over more and more of the work. There were some specialist tasks, such as plate laying, which the French initially found difficult, but in time they mastered that art as well. In the early days it had been the British workers who had earned the admiration of all who watched them. This was a description of navvies at work as seen by one of Brassey's timekeepers:

> I think as fine a spectacle as any man can witness, who is accustomed to look at work, is to see a cutting in full operation, with about twenty wagons being filled, every man at his post, and every man with his shirt open, working in the heat of the day, the gangers looking about, and everything going like clockwork. Such an exhibition of physical power attracted many French gentlemen, who came on to the cuttings at Paris and Rouen, and looking at these English workmen with astonishment, said, 'Mon Dieu! Les Anglais, comme ils travaillent!' Another thing that called forth remark, was the complete silence that prevailed amongst the men. It was a fine sight to see the Englishmen that were there, with their muscular arms and hands hairy and brown.

There was one area in particular where British expertise and experience was all important, and that was in the construction of tunnels. The navvies were able to endure the often terrible conditions, working all day with shirts saturated with water and breathing a foul atmosphere. The conditions in a tunnel could easily intimidate the novice. As timbers were inserted to shore up the roof, they creaked and groaned under the weight of the earth above them, and it must have seemed like the whole tunnel could cave in at any moment. Charles Jones, one of the men in charge of tunnelling, was asked if the British navvy had to have special qualities:

> Yes; it is often necessary to strengthen the temporary timber structures by adding additional beams, or placing uprights underneath the planks overhead, which are yielding to the weight above them. It requires a considerable amount of courage in the men employed in this kind of work. If they shrink from facing a certain amount of danger, the whole structure would sometimes come in upon them, thereby endangering their lives, and retarding very considerably the progress of the works.[9]

Helps's biography is necessarily more about its subject than about the men he employed, and we are lucky that he took so much trouble to find out about and record the lives of the navvies. The Mackenzie Papers are different. They consist mainly of the diaries kept by the two brothers; they were never intended for publication and simply record events as they happened on a day-to-day basis. Edward, the younger brother, was very much the man on the spot. He set up his office in France, brought his family over and stayed on through the whole construction period – on the Paris to Rouen line and then, from 1843, on the Rouen to Le Havre line.

Many of the problems the contractors faced were those common to any railway construction site. For a start there were the inevitable delays. January 1842 proved a troublesome month. On the 4th, Edward was up early and made his way to woodland where he found a large gang hanging about with nothing to do, simply because the paperwork for acquiring the land had not come through. Edward managed to find a spot where a patch of land had been acquired and set the men to work digging a gully; he then went home for breakfast. By the 7th the land was acquired and the men were able to get on with setting out the line, but by the 10th it had all more or less come to a stop, due to a severe frost which had got 'deep into the ground'. A few men strug-gled on, but very little was done. The frost lasted for a week and they didn't get going again until the 17th. The rest of the month was comparatively unevent-ful, apart from a minor fracas. One of the Frenchmen hit an English overseer, Mr Rhodes, on the 20th. He reported to the office the following day to collect his pay and was 'very insolent' and Edward 'put him out of the yard'. Once the entire affair had been settled, the local mayor turned up with a gendarme, too late to be of any use. A good deal of the Mackenzies' time was taken up with trying to co-ordinate the work to make sure everything ran smoothly.

In February 1843 the workers at Poissy were having to labour flat out under very difficult conditions in order to allow the ballasters to move forward. Other delays must have been all too familiar to the railway contractors. A typical note read: 'very few men at work being pay Monday'. Tuesday was not much better.

Pay presented its own problems. The system was the usual one in which the contractors paid subcontractors and gangers, who were responsible for paying the men. And, as always, there was the risk of the ganger taking the money and disappearing – 'sloping' as it was known. On 25 April 1842 Mackenzie received a report that a ganger called Lamours had been paid 5,300 francs and had disappeared. The following day the gang appeared demanding their money: 'We sent them off.' This was standard British practice: the contrac-tors had paid the money to the appropriate person and as far as they were concerned that was that. The men thought differently. The next day Edward was on his way to another part of the line when he was met by a group of the discontented navvies; they grabbed hold of him and told him that he would be held hostage until they were paid. In the event, he was rescued by the Dragoons after just a few hours in captivity. To prevent matters getting any worse, the contractors agreed to refer the matter to arbitrators, and again the British must have felt confident in the result. The contractors, however, were dealing with French lawyers not English magistrates. They discovered the dif-ference on 27 May:

The Tribunal decided today that we have to pay Lamours men but they said we were not bound but for to keep peace it was better to pay them. They said this is French law – the people are masters not the Magistrates. We had to pay to the men 7120 francs – this sum is now twice paid.

The contractors were now a bit more cautious. In August that year there were some doubts about a Belgian ganger, so they went along to see the men and asked them if they were confident they would get their money. They all said there would be no problem so the cash was paid out to the ganger. The next day they were just sitting down to dinner when a deputation turned up: 'The Belgian had sloped after all the precautions we had taken.' Edward had rather better luck when working on the Orleans railway. He heard that a ganger called Simcox had sloped and he reasoned that he was most likely to be heading back to England. He was caught just as he was about to board a coach for Paris, hauled back to the office, where he handed over all the money – 1,300 francs. He was sacked and sent away penniless to make his way home as best he could.

Another recurring feature in the diaries is the recording of accidents, of the kind all too familiar from the worksites back in Britain, such as this one on 10 November 1846: 'An English driver on top of the said cutting ... was killed today by the wagon running over him caused by getting his foot fast in the points when going in with a full wagon.' Navvies suffering serious injuries were repatriated and, in accordance with French law, were paid compensation. Edward accompanied one of these men, known as Irish Pete, for part of the way, but found him 'very insolent'. As he had just had both arms shattered and lost his sight, he might be excused for feeling a bit irritable.

On the whole the work went forward well. William Mackenzie undercut French contractors to obtain the contract for building the Baranton viaduct on the line from Rouen to Le Havre. It was an immense affair: 100ft high, a third of a mile long and carried on twenty-seven arches. To get the contract he bid what he described as '6 per cent too low' at just over 2 million francs – roughly £800,000. There was a disagreement between the contractor and the engineer Locke about the type of mortar to be used. Mackenzie favoured the more expensive hydraulic mortar, but Locke merely said that he could use it if he pleased but there would be no extra allowance in the costings. On 12 January 1846, the entire structure collapsed. There could have been extensive litigation, but Brassey and Mackenzie made no attempt to shift the blame. They at once agreed to rebuild it, and the following day Brassey met with Locke to discuss the plans. They bore the full costs themselves.

Apart from the catastrophe at Baranton, most of the problems faced by the two Mackenzie brothers would have been familiar enough, but nothing in their experience could have prepared them for the events of 1848, in what became known as 'The Year of Revolutions'. Edward's diaries recorded the events as he witnessed them, starting on 24 February, when he described conditions in Paris, where the king had abdicated, barricades had gone up in the streets and people were calling for a republic. Soon enough the troubles spread to the railway. The first signs of local trouble appeared in March, when a number of mechanics were prevented from arriving at the works by 'the Revolutionaries'. Trouble erupted a week later at a tunnel, where the brick-layers were pelted with bricks and told to leave. The men refused to go back to work, saying they were in fear of their lives, even though two gendarmes appeared who promised to protect them. This, it turned out, was just a minor problem compared with what was to happen the following month. The gov-ernment announced that they were taking over all railway works themselves, and that the contractors were to be paid off. There was nothing to do but to pack up all the equipment, draw money to pay off the men and go home. Edward, however, simply moved across the border to new works in Belgium.

A young engineer called William Lloyd, who had only completed his engi-neering apprenticeship in 1838, managed to get himself appointed to what was known as 'the Great Northern of France' as resident engineer.[10] By now, the British navvy presence was reduced to a few key men who were there to show the locals how to do things. Lloyd and six men arrived at Beaumont eager to start work, but there was nothing and no one there to get them started: no tools, no men, no anything. Baffled, he asked his employers what he should do, and they replied with what Lloyd described as a 'peremptory order' to find 300 men from somewhere and get on with it. He put up notices asking the locals to volunteer for work and to bring with them any useful tools they happened to own. Not knowing what to expect, he turned up at the meeting place to be confronted by 'a motley crowd of volunteer navvies, numbering more than a hundred, with every species of earth-disturbing implement, and with a perfect collection of wheelbarrows, many of remote antiquity'. He set the band to work as best they could, but he was greatly relieved when a band of professional Belgian navvies appeared on site looking for jobs, all of whom had already worked on the railways. He put them to work at once, thinking his troubles were over. He was wrong: they were just about to start.

The French did not want Belgians working on their line and threatened to kill any of them who even tried to pick up a shovel. Lloyd went to the French to try to reason with them, but the more he said the angrier they got. One of the English navvies, known as Tom Breakwater because he was born during the construction of the Plymouth breakwater, came over to see what the fuss was about. Lloyd explained that they were threatening to throw him in the river, which didn't seem to worry Tom very much, who simply said, 'Never mind, master, I'll pull you out.' Lloyd was not impressed with this plan and came up with a far better idea to calm everyone down. He announced that he wouldn't discuss the issue at the moment because he had just heard that this was a King's Fete day, and everyone could take the day off. Instead of booing, the crowd cheered and everyone was happy. Lloyd went off to the nearest inn to recover, where he found the ringleaders who had threatened to dunk him enjoying their wine. They greeted him like an old friend, and they spent the rest of the day together drinking the King's health.

Lloyd, like many other British engineers, spent a great deal of his time travelling around the world constructing railways. Tom Breakwater also went wandering across the continents to find work. They met again in very different circumstances in 1853. Lloyd had set off for Chile with his wife and two children, having been recommended to the Chilean government by Robert Stephenson. The journey proved rather more troublesome than he expected. The journey to New York by paddle steamer was uneventful, but when he got there he found gaining a passage to South America was almost impossible as the Californian Gold Rush was still at its height. There was not yet a rail connection across the continent, so the only options were either to take a ship round Cape Horn or go to Panama and risk the fever-infected land route across the isthmus. Eventually, they managed to get a berth on a pensioned-off and once very grand yacht that had originally belonged to the Vanderbilts, which took them as far as Panama; from here they managed to get a more conventional passage to Valparaíso. Among the passengers was his old navvy companion Tom Breakwater, heading for work in Peru. But he had succumbed to fever in Panama, and within a day of setting sail, he died.

The story of Lloyd and Tom Breakwater is just one of many that involve engineers, contractors and navvies from Britain working all round the world. The obvious locations for navvy involvement were those where British influence was strongest, and paramount among them was India. The case for railways was easily made; one engineer noted that India was not like England, where railways had simply been an improvement on the earlier roads and canals – in India they would be 'the first introduction of any communication whatever'. Stories of travel on the muddy tracks that passed as main roads were legion. A civil servant, for example, set off on a journey, during which his driver told him an account of a previous passenger who had been so shaken by a sudden jolt that he had bitten off the end of his tongue. The lack of good communication was highlighted during the First Sikh War, when all the officers in Calcutta were told to report immediately to the north-west frontier for duty. It took them so long to get there that the war had finished by the time they arrived.

The development of the Indian railway system was hampered by the cumbersome bureaucracy and problems with raising the necessary finance. Even when work did get under way, the necessity of referring all decisions back to Britain made life difficult and often produced absurd results. In 1853, when a new booking office and goods shed were required in Bombay (now Mumbai), instead of being made locally they were prefabricated in iron in Britain and then shipped out to India. Not surprisingly, working in a cast-iron shed in the middle of an Indian summer was a total nightmare. Just to make matters worse in getting a comprehensive railway system established, there was a long discussion on what gauge to use: some favoured the Stephenson version of 4ft 8½in; others argued for Brunel's more generous 7ft. A compromise was reached at 5ft 6in, but when money grew short a new generation of lines was constructed to metre gauge. India finished up with the curse of the mixed gauge, to which narrow gauge was later added in the hills. Progress was painfully slow, but in 1853 a modest 20-mile route was opened along the coastal plain from Bombay to Thala. It was described by the Indian paper *Overland Telegraph and Carrier* as 'a triumph, to which in comparison all our victories in the east seem tame and commonplace'. The Governor of Bombay and other dignitaries seem to have been less impressed, as they never even bothered to turn up for the opening ceremonies – the weather was hot so they went for their customary stay in the cool of the hill stations instead. It was a start, and another line was already under construction to the east, but far greater challenges lay ahead.

One of the main jobs on the Indus Valley State Railway was the construction of a bridge across the River Sutlej. As at similar sites in Britain, a shantytown for the workforce grew up that at one time held up to 6,000 people. The main problem, however, was not accidents, but disease, which led to an engineer reporting that three out of four workmen were laid up with fever. When the protecting bank broke and much of the site was flooded, the resulting distress made things even worse, and it was estimated that 1,000 died of pneumonia. But for a line that combined immense engineering difficulties with a hostile terrain, nothing compared to the task of constructing the line to link Bombay on the coast to the towns and cities of the central plateau. In between lay the Western Ghats, cliffs that rise to a height of 2,500ft. Even today, going up the road is a major undertaking: trucks crawl up the zigzagging route and the roadside is littered with the wrecks of those that failed to make it. To build a railway up the Ghats presented a problem for which European railway construction offered no precedents. The only answer was steep gradients that ranged from 1 in 48 to 1 in 37, but that was only achieved by using the same technique as that used on the road, building the line in a zigzag. But as trains could not make their way round hairpin bends, reversing stations had to be provided at the end of each incline. This enabled the train to continue on past the end of the slope, reverse, and carry on up the next slope travelling in the opposite direction. There were, in fact, two main inclines up the Thul Ghat and the Bhore Ghat, the latter being 15½ miles long with a total rise of 2,000ft, twenty-five tunnels and twenty-two bridges. It would have been a Herculean task anywhere in the world, but in India, with a mainly untrained workforce and terrible conditions, it was truly daunting.

The engineering staff was British, the contractors who took on much of the work were British, and some navvies came with them. They had no knowledge of local conditions and some rapidly succumbed. Solomon Treadwell took out a contract and arrived in Bombay on 15 September 1855.

Two weeks later he had died of fever, at which point his stalwart wife took over the contract and saw it through to completion. The navvies who came to India behaved much as they had anywhere else in the world. One group was having a great time when a group of local policemen appeared to try to restore order: 'Each navvy took two constables, one under each arm, and chucked them outside the railway fence.'[11]

Many of the British navvies found working in the tropical conditions intolerable, but some stayed on. There were areas where their expertise was essential. For example, there was no tradition of tunnelling in India and certain jobs, such as timbering, were always their responsibility. Others stayed on as gangers: they were under strict instructions, issued by Sir Bartle Frere from the governor's office, not to strike a native. Anyone found doing so would forfeit their return fare, paid for by the company, and be dismissed. But when Frere came on a tour of inspection and met a 'big, brawny navvy' it seemed the instructions had not percolated down to ground level:

'Well, my good man, you appear to be the manager here.'
'Yes, Sir,' was the reply.
'And how are you getting on?'
'Oh, Sir, we are getting on very well.'
'How many natives have you under your orders?'
'Well, Sir, about 500 on 'em altogether.'
'Do you speak their language?'
'No, Sir, I don't.'
'Well then, how do you manage to let these natives understand what they are to do?'
'Oh, Sir, I'll tell you. I tell these chaps three times in good plain English, and then if they don't understand that, I takes the lukri [stick] and we get on very well.'[12]

It turned out the navvy was not a brutal overseer at all, but simply a man with a sense of humour who liked sending up officialdom, and was mainly noted for being kind-hearted. It was not brutality from overseers that most affected the Indian workers. They suffered their share of accidents, particularly when dealing with such unfamiliar operations as blasting, but as at the Sutlej site, it was disease that was the real killer. The British engineers seemed rather more concerned with the delays in construction than the death toll:

The fine season of eight months is favourable for Indian railway operations, but, on the other hand, fatal epidemics, such as cholera and fever, often break out, and the labourers are, generally, of such a feeble constitution, and so badly provided with shelter and clothing, that they speedily succumb to these diseases, and the benefits of the fine weather are, thereby temporarily lost.[13]

It is a statement that hardly reflects well on British attitudes. If the men were badly housed and clothed, then who was to blame? No exact statistics were kept, but it was estimated that thousands lost their lives before the Ghats were conquered. Nowhere else the British navvy went in his search for work produced fatalities on such a scale, though many had their own unique problems.

Indian railway workers were given the opportunity to emulate their British counterparts by going overseas to work. The Kenya & Uganda Railway was to stretch from Mombasa to Lake Victoria and was fraught with difficulties from the inception, when the surveying party suffered everything from attacks by the local Masai to being charged at by a rhinoceros. When it came to building the line, the company found the Africans had very little interest in the work; even those who did sign up were liable to wander away if they decided they needed to plant or harvest crops at home, so advertisements for workers were placed in Bombay. The Indian government only allowed recruitment if assurances were given that the men would receive a regular, decent wage and at the end of a three-year contract they either had to be paid the expenses to get home or allowed to settle in Kenya. The first 350 arrived in Mombasa in 1897 and before the line was completed it was estimated that some 30,000 Indian navvies had been employed. What none of them could have realised was that a unique terror awaited them at one of the construction sites.

Tsavo was the site of a major project to build a bridge across the river, and soon a huge encampment developed there. One night, seven men were sleeping in one of the tents when a lion burst in, grabbed a Sikh called Ungan Singh and dragged him away. Next day his dismembered body was found, of which only the head, with wide-open, staring eyes, was intact. The lions hunted in pairs and as time went on they got ever bolder and more and more men were killed. There was panic in the camp: some demanded to be taken away on the supply train; some managed to sleep up trees and in water towers, while others dug pits in their tents, crept into them and put logs on top – which must have been a nightmarish way to spend a sultry African night, but better than being eaten alive. The man in charge on the site was Lieutenant Colonel J.H. Patterson, and he came up with what he thought was a brilliant idea.[14] He constructed a huge trap and put two 'coolies' inside as bait. They would be separated from the lions by a wooden gate at the end of the cage, and each supplied with guns to finish the beasts off. The lions duly arrived, but the terrified men shot in all directions and the lions escaped. It was said they almost shot Patterson, but that may not have been accidental: one might not think too kindly of a man who had volunteered you as bait for man-eaters. Patterson himself was a keen hunter and he managed to shoot a lion or two, but the problem was only really resolved when the camp moved on.

Very few, if any, British navvies were employed in Africa, but one group did make a major contribution to what was arguably the most ambitious and difficult railway construction work of them all: the line that was to be built across America to join the west coast to the east. The story of this line is one of contrasting elements, from fraud and greed to heroic endeavour. The work was divided between two companies: the Central Pacific that was to start in California at Sacramento, and had the difficult job of first conquering the Sierra mountains, and the Union Pacific that began in Omaha, Nebraska, and had the somewhat easier job of crossing the great central plains. The line had been authorised and was paid for by the government which, to encourage rapid progress, made a grant of United States Bonds for every 40 miles of track completed, as well as grants to the land on either side of the line. This generosity was based on the assumption that the land was theirs to give away, and there was a nod to the fact that some people actually lived there already. That was easily dealt with by a rider specifying that the government would 'extinguish as rapidly as may be the Indian titles to all lands falling under the operations of this act'. This scheme was to lead to all kinds of trouble and had consequences that were not foreseen by its initiators. An example occurred at the start of work at Omaha. The conscientious chief engineer, Peter Dey, planned the first part of the route in 1864 and put in his estimates. Thomas Durant who ran Union Pacific promptly increased them to get more cash from the government and appointed a new engineer over Dey's head. The new man changed the route, for no obvious engineering reason, increasing the first section from 23 miles to 32. This brought in not only extra US Bonds but acquired land that would be increasingly valuable as Omaha expanded. Dey resigned in disgust. Similar disgraceful stories besmirch the history of the Union Pacific. The whole story of the enterprise is fascinating, and this history has a direct bearing on the life of the navvies who built the line.[15]

The main workforce for the Union Pacific was made up of Irish navvies, many of whom had probably gained their early experience on the other side of the Atlantic. The Central Pacific had greater difficulty recruiting workers. In California there was much more interest in digging for gold than there was in digging railroads, so the company had the bright idea of importing workers from China. When someone suggested they were too puny a race for a task of this size, the engineer pointed out that a race that could build the Great Wall of China could build anything. So at one end of the line the Chinese laboured through the mountains, blasting tunnels and facing immense difficulties, while the Irish steadily pushed their line towards them.

Samuel Bowles, publisher of the *Springfield Republican*, wrote an account of the navvy towns that developed along the route:

As the Railroad marched thus rapidly across the broad Continent of plain and mountain, there was improvised a rough and temporary town at its every public stopping place ... these settlements were of the most perishable materials – canvas tents, plain board shanties, and turf-hovels – pulled down and sent forward for a new career, or deserted as worthless, at every grand movement of the Railroad company … Restaurant and saloon keepers, gamblers, desperadoes of every kind, the vilest of men and women made up this Hell on Wheels.

These were the rough towns that began the legends of the Wild West, where men swaggered around with pistols at their belts and were ready to use them. It was claimed that more Union Pacific navvies were murdered in the camps than died in accidents. By comparison, the riotous British navvy must have seemed comparatively tame. One constant remained: the hard work of the men. A newspaper reporter left a lengthy description of how the tracks advanced. Unlike at European construction sites, there was no overall detailed survey of the whole route carried out in advance. The surveyors moved in the vanguard, marking out the line, to be followed by the 'graders'. These were the men who where necessary dug cuttings, built embankments and bridges. Construction trains kept pace with the workings. The first was the supply train, with a string of boxcars fitted out with bunks and acting as temporary accommodation for the navvies. After that was the equipment train, carrying ties (sleepers), rails and spikes, which were dropped off beside the finished track. Horse-drawn carts then took the material on to the advancing railhead. What followed was a well-organised system:

> Two men grasp the forward end of the rail and start ahead with it, the rest of the gang taking hold two by two, until it is clear of the car. At the word of command it is dropped into place, right side up, during which a similar operation has been going with the rail from the other side – thirty seconds to the rail for each gang, four rails to the minute … Close behind the track-layers come the gaugers, then the spikers and bolters. Three strokes to the spike, ten spikes to the rail, four hundred rails to the mile. Quick work, you might think – but the fellows of the Union Pacific are tremendously in earnest.

Just how fast the work could be done was demonstrated on 28 April 1869 when a specially selected team of eight Irishmen laid and spiked 1 mile of track in a day. Their names deserve to be recorded – Dailey, Elliott, Joyce, Kennedy, Killeen, McNamara, Shay and Sullivan.

As the two sets of tracks approached each other from east and west, the competition became fierce. Each company wanted to lay as many miles as possible to gain the government bonuses of land and bonds. The situation was taken to absurd lengths. The two refused to make a junction, and continued to drive on past each other. The rival workforces were encouraged not only to work faster and faster, but do their best to slow down the opposition. At one point, the two routes were very close together, with the Irish at one level and the Chinese slightly higher up. The Irish took to blasting without any warning, and the Chinese eventually retaliated with far more serious results – the men at the lower level were buried under an avalanche of spoil. At this point the two groups decided that, whatever their masters might want to do, they would call a truce. Eventually sense prevailed and the lines were joined at Promontory, Utah, in 1869.

Further north in Canada, railway development was comparatively slow and depended heavily on English contractors and the men they brought with them. There were plenty of volunteers because the pay was good, far better than back home. Navvies were paid 4s a day and skilled workers could make as much as 10s. Some of the work on the Grand Trunk Railway was taken by Brassey. He came over in person to see how things were progressing and suggested that more men were needed and they should recruit French Canadians. It was not an entirely successful experiment:

> They could ballast, but they could not excavate. They could not even ballast as the English navvy does, continuously working at 'filling' for the whole day. The only way in which they could be worked was by allowing them to fill the wagons, and then ride out with the ballast train to the place where the ballast was tipped, giving them an opportunity of resting. Then the empty wagons went back again to be filled; and so, alternately resting during the work, in that way, they did very much more. They could work fast for ten minutes and they were 'done'. This was not through idleness, but physical weakness. They are small men and they are a class who are not well fed. They live entirely on vegetable food, and they scarcely ever taste meat.[16]

Even with the addition of the French Canadians, who mostly worked under English gangers, there were never enough men, so the contractors brought in steam excavators. Mr Rowan, the engineer on the spot, was not very impressed with the mechanical navvies. He conceded they were useful in 'hard stuff', but when it came to loose soil or gravel, it was cheaper to pay men, even at the rate of 5 or 6s a day.

The biggest challenge facing the engineers was the construction of a bridge across the St Lawrence River. The engineer was Robert Stephenson and he decided to use the same tubular construction that had proved so successful on the Holyhead line. This, however, was on a far larger scale: the Menai Bridge had been considered a major achievement at 1,800ft, but the tubes for the St Lawrence crossing were to consist of twenty-five spans, with a total length of 6,512ft. The job was made slightly simpler by the fact that the river was comparatively shallow and ran over rock that would provide a firm foundation for the piers. Even so, it was an immense undertaking and at one time over 3,000 men were at work.

The first temporary dam was started in May 1854, and a familiar pattern began of floating out caissons, pumping them dry and working inside them to build the foundations for the piers. There was one difference, however, in that they had to remove the caissons each winter to protect them from the ice floes that thundered down the river. Inevitably, this slowed work down, but the biggest problem was caused by disease and climate. The workers who had come from England suffered greatly. They had never experienced anything like the cold of a Canadian winter and many men suffered from frostbite, while the fine snow blowing in their faces and the harsh white glare could cause temporary blindness. Summer brought diseases, such as cholera, from which many men never recovered. The bridge was finally completed on 24 November 1859, six weeks after Stephenson's death.

Canadians, like the natives of other countries that had relied on British expertise in the early years, soon realised that not only could they manage without the help, the advice was not always appropriate for the very different conditions. For example, Americans spiked their rails directly into the wooden sleepers, while the British set their rails in metal chairs for greater rigidity. The trouble was that in the extreme cold of Canadian winters, the rigid British system was more likely to produce cracking than the flexible American version. Add to that the fact that the chairs had to be sent over from England at considerable expense and people started to wonder whether they should follow the American example. It did not take long to arrive at the conclusion that they might be better doing things their own way. The days of English contractors and navvies were over.

Labour problems were a major factor in the early years of railway development in Canada, and they were even more pressing on the other side of the world in Australia. Once again, Brassey was one of the main contractors, though he never travelled there himself. The job of organising the workforce went to one of his trusted agents, Samuel Wilcox. He described how Brassey recruited men in Britain by selecting some 2,000 from among the ranks of known, reliable navvies.[17] These were not men who were expected to do the job and return home afterwards. Wilcox explained that the navvies were well paid at from 7 to 8s a week and provisions were comparatively cheap: 'As long as a man with a family is kept from drink there, he can, in a very short time, get enough money to start and buy a piece of land, and become settled.' The proviso about drink was crucial, for although some things were cheap, beer was expensive. When Brassey had recruited the men, he had to provide each of them with an outfit, according to government regulations, which cost £5 per man, and contribute £12 towards the passage, so that he was paying out around £34,000:

> 'We sacrificed that', Mr. Wilcox says, 'to get the men there. Having men in the country, we knew that they must work for somebody; and we also knew that we were in a position to pay them as much as, or more than, any one else. They were at liberty, on landing, to go where they liked; and some few, not a great number, but some few, never came to the works at all; but we found that we got a great part of them, and many more came by other ships.'

So, as in so many other countries around the world, Australia's railways were helped on their way by the British navvy. A regular pattern emerged of work being started by British contractors and navvies, but eventually being taken over by the locals. Back in Britain, the network had developed rapidly and as more and more places were connected, so the whole building process began to slow down. By the end of the nineteenth century, it was almost complete, but there were still two major projects to keep the navvies at work.

CHAPTER THIRTEEN

THE END OF THE LINE

Towards the end of the nineteenth century, the railway map of Britain was filling up and it must have seemed to many navvies that the time had come to start thinking about a new occupation. Then two major projects came along, both creating huge demands for labour. The first takes us right back to the beginning of the navvy story, with the construction of a waterway to link Manchester and Liverpool, but on a scale that the Duke of Bridgewater could never have imagined. This was the Manchester Ship Canal. It was not only far bigger than the Bridgewater Canal, but in order to complete it the engineers would have to demolish the latter's most iconic landmark, the Barton aqueduct. The plans of the engineer Leader Williams called for the canalisation of the River Irwell and as ships would never be able to pass under the aqueduct it had to be replaced. The solution was to build an ingenious swing aqueduct. The iron trough pivots on a central pier. When vessels need to use the ship canal, the trough and the canal are both closed off by watertight gates at either end. Then the trough is swung, still full of water, so that instead of crossing the river at right angles, it comes to rest in a position aligned to the banks. This leaves ample space for ships to pass on either side of the central pier. The impressive feature of the canal is its sheer size: the biggest locks are 600ft by 65ft and the canal itself has a maximum depth of 120ft. This feat of engineering was not going to be achieved merely by men with spades and wheelbarrows. All the latest available technology was brought in to help with the work.

The statistics for the construction period, which lasted from 1887 to 1893, give a good idea of the scale of the works. Steam excavators were brought over from France and Germany, complete with their French and German operators. It was all a great contrast to the days when the world looked to Britain for the latest technology, though some British 'steam navvies' were also used. When everything was up and running, there were over a hundred of these machines puffing and blowing along the canal. There was a variety of different devices used for getting the spoil up from the bed of the canal to the bank. These included a type of funicular railway consisting of wheeled platforms, each able to take a couple of carts, and a steam-powered conveyor belt. The most impressive feature of all was the railway, where spoil wagons ran on 223 miles of track, with an astonishing 173 locomotives used for haulage. It was the biggest private railway in the country. Added to all this were varieties of crane, steam pumps and portable engines. Yet in spite of the machinery, there was still an immense workforce, with up to 16,000 men and boys on the job. The main contract was held by Thomas Walker, a man we have already met when he was in charge of the Severn Tunnel.

In spite of the degree of mechanisation involved, the jobs would have been familiar to the railway navvies. Unlike the earlier canals, the Manchester Ship Canal construction began in the age of photography and there are some remarkable pictures of the actual workings. In one photograph, you can see the rail tracks, packed with wagons, a line that disappears into the distance, and each truck has a gang of men at work, filling it. Other photos show more details of the work, and one can see just how high the men had to throw the spoil to fill a truck. To stabilise the banks, wooden pegs were driven into the slope and willow twigs wound round to provide a protective cover, work that must have been more welcome than the endless loading of railway trucks. There are also photographs of some of the people who came to the sites to try to make some money. One man has buckets of coffee to sell to the workers. Another man stands outside a rough shelter, built out of sleepers, with tin mugs and jugs of liquor. The company actively encouraged the former and discouraged the latter as far as it could. The accident rate was alarmingly high, with 130 fatalities and over 3,000 serious injuries: the injured were known ironically as 'Walker's Fragments'. The company blamed it all on drunkenness, rather than any intrinsic dangers in the works. Things were so bad that a Liverpool surgeon, Sir Robert Jones, set up three hospitals along the line and a number of smaller first-aid posts. They not only dealt with accidents but also coped with the numerous diseases that were the inevitable consequence of the poor, often insanitary living conditions.

No wage books or records have survived, but there was a census taken during the construction which listed men who were in lodgings, and they seem mostly to have been Irish. One farm labourer's family, themselves from Ireland, took in ten 'Ship Canal Labourers'. There was never going to be enough space available in local cottages, and most of the rest were housed in what came to be known as 'tin towns' – temporary villages that were built at four sites along the canal. They were very basic, served by a rough main road, with open gutters all down the sides, crossed by bare planks that provided access to the houses. One of these settlements at Marshville was provided with a mission hall and a 200-seat coffee house. A family that took one of these huts often took in lodgers, the wife doing all the cooking and charging 13s a week

for bed and board.¹ There were other more makeshift arrangements, including a 'floating hotel', which seems to have been no more than a rough shelter
erected on top of a barge.

The Ship Canal Company produced regular statistics about the amount of
work done by the machines and the men. The report for 1894 gave figures
of 76 million tons of spoil having been shifted, of which a fifth was rock.
Construction used up 175,000 cubic yards of bricks, such a vast amount that
they built their own brickworks; and 220,000 cubic yards of masonry was built,
much of the rock coming out of the excavation. A material that was still new
to this type of work in Britain, even though it had been used by the Romans
centuries earlier, made an even bigger contribution: 1,250,000 cubic yards of
cement was used. The Manchester Ship Canal was one of the great achieve-
ments of Victorian engineering, but it was to be the last major undertaking
on any British canal. There was, however, still to be one important main-line
railway to be constructed.

The Great Central Railway was not really one railway at all, but an amalgam
of a number of different companies, stemming right back to the early years
with the line from Sheffield to Manchester that included the famous, or infa-
mous, Woodhead Tunnel. By 1847, new lines had been added to form what
was now called the Manchester, Sheffield & Lincolnshire Railway. The company was regularly beset with financial difficulties, but when Edward Watkin
took over as chairman he instituted a number of bold new plans for expansion.
The boldest of them all proved a little too ambitious.

Watkin was chair of the Metropolitan, East London and South Eastern
Railways and the optimistically named Channel Tunnel Company, and his
ultimate ambition was a through route from Manchester to Paris. In the event,
the company settled for the more manageable plan of continuing their network down as far as London. The route ran through Nottingham, Leicester
and Rugby to Quainton Road, where it joined the Metropolitan Railway
that was already in place and carried the line as far as St John's Wood in North
London. From there the line was intended to continue under the turf of Lord's
cricket ground, committing the ultimate sacrilege. The final section would
end at a new main-line station at St Marylebone. The Act was approved in
1893, in spite of fierce opposition from the existing London lines from the
Midlands, not to mention irate cricketers. It was only after reaching the capital
that the name was changed to Great Central.

The engineers had the advantage of decades of railway construction to build
on, unlike Robert Stephenson when he had been in charge of the first connecting link between London and the Midlands. They built for high-speed
travel. If a curve was necessary, they made sure it was a gentle one. The land is
far from flat between Quainton Road and Leicester, but the ruling gradient
was kept to a modest 1 in 176. Inevitably this involved considerable earthworks
and, as on the Manchester Ship Canal, mechanical steam navvies were brought

in to help. The six contractors who worked on the line had thirty-nine of these machines, each of which it was said could do the work of a hundred men. But although the mechanical diggers were fine for roughing out the line of a cutting, the work still needed to be completed by navvies. And, of course, they also still had the job of loading spoil into the contractors' trains.

As with the Manchester Ship Canal there is an extensive pictorial record of the works, thanks to one enthusiastic local photographer, S. W. A. Newton.[2] He shot pictures of the working sites, and there are dramatic views that give one a clear idea of just what a blot on the landscape a new railway could be, particularly when slicing through the chalk hills, where cuttings appear as startling white scars. Newton was just as interested in the life of the navvies as he was in the works, and he took many photographs that show aspects of their lives that seldom appear in earlier accounts. A number of villages were built along the line, each consisting of soundly built wooden cabins with corrugated metal roofs. There were dormitories for the single men and individual cabins for families. It is possible that Newton chose the best examples to photograph, but those he did are notable for being positively homely. The interior of a foreman's hut has an ornate iron bedstead, a rug on the floor, a table with ornaments and a picture on the wall; a pram stands in one corner of the room. Some of the occupants even made gardens where they grew their own vegetables. It is not clear how many of the 10,000 men who worked on the line were housed in these temporary villages, but those who were enjoyed a perfectly acceptable standard of living, certainly compared with the many slums that still blighted the industrial cities at the end of the nineteenth century.

Newton seems to have had a special interest in the work of the various navvy missions that were set up. Like the houses, these were mainly quite primitive wooden structures, built to the same standard as the cabins. There was also a navvies' reading room, with simple wooden benches, and a little whitewashed cottage was turned into The Navvy Mission Good Samaritan House, where navvies on the tramp were given a night's accommodation for free. One photograph shows a Sunday school outing, with children gathered under a Navvy Mission banner and a brass band behind them. The children and their parents all look to be well dressed in their Sunday best. It is about as far from the old picture of the roistering, riotous navvy as one could imagine. But it was not quite the whole picture.

The line had to make its way through Nottingham in a tunnel. The city is famous for its complex of old cellars; so many of them that no one knew what would turn up as the work proceeded. Under the Guildhall they broke into an old dungeon that contained the macabre remains of executed criminals. Far more to the navvies' liking was the discovery of the cellar of the Old Cross Keys Inn, full of wine and beer. It did not remain full of drink for long: there was a limit to the influence of the Navvy Missions and their temperance crusades.

When the work was finally completed in 1899 it marked the end of an era. There were to be no more major main-line routes built in Britain until the end of the twentieth century, with the construction of the new rail link to the Channel Tunnel. Railway construction did not come to an abrupt conclusion. There were still improvements to be made to earlier lines, branch lines to be constructed and a whole new type of railway to be built to fill in some of the gaps in the existing system. In 1896 the government passed the Light Railways Act.[3] This cut away a lot of the red tape that hampered the construction of railways, allowed for less demanding standards in construction, but offset these advantages by imposing a speed limit of 25mph. The whole essence of a light railway was that it should be cheap, as it was never expected to raise a large revenue, simply because it seldom visited any large centres of population. The whole idea was to provide the benefits of the railway to communities that were too small to interest the big companies. In practice, this meant cutting costs to the absolute minimum: reducing earthworks to as few as possible, using light rails and not worrying too much about tight bends since all the trains were going slowly anyway. An example is the Basingstoke to Alton line, which was only built in the first place by the London & South Western Railway to block the ambitions of the Great Western, who were planning to open a route that looked likely to threaten the LSWR's Portsmouth traffic. The entire cost for the 13-mile route was only £67,000, achieved by keeping the line almost entirely on the level. This meant missing out most of the intervening villages, though Cliddesdon did manage to acquire a station half a mile away but that, like others along the route, was a rough affair of corrugated iron. There were just three trains a day and even these failed to achieve the statutory speed limit, only averaging 13mph and some of the curves had 10mph boards at the track-side. Not surprisingly, it was never a commercial success. Such a line was never going to call on the services of a large workforce. But not every line was this modest, and some at least had major engineering features.

The Bere Alston & Calstock Light Railway was an extension of the line from Plymouth to Calstock, and it faced one formidable obstacle. It had to cross the deep Tamar valley. The man in charge was Colonel Holman Fred Stephens, probably the most influential figure in the whole light railway movement. In earlier years this enterprise would have involved quarrying huge quantities of stone or providing equally vast numbers of bricks, but Stephens went for a more modern material: concrete. The viaduct across the river is 1,000ft long and 117ft high, and a grand total of 11,148 blocks of concrete were used to build it. It was, and is, a magnificent structure and still in use – unlike many light railways. The Bideford, Westward Ho & Appledore Railway, for example, opened in 1901 and by 1917 it was closed. There were some forty lines built under the Act, right up to the 1920s, but they all had the same characteristics of being comparatively short, cheap and not requiring a very large workforce in their construction. They gave employment to some navvies, but never enough to keep the tens of thousands of men who were experienced but unemployed. Where did the rest go? There were other major construction sites in the country, notably a number of large reservoirs that still needed massed forces of manual labourers, and it made very little difference to the navvy whether the large hole he was digging was going to be a ship canal or filled with water for drinking. But as the twentieth century advanced, so the demand simply fell away, and even big construction projects that were begun were increasingly mechanised. For all practical purposes, the great age of the navvy ended with the close of the nineteenth century.

There had always been endings in the life of a navvy. Whenever a railway or canal was finished, he had to go off to find new work, but at least he generally left in style. There was usually some splendid ceremony to mark the day that the new transport route was officially opened, and the navvies often had a part in it. A typical example from the canal age would be the ceremony to mark the opening of the Pontcysyllte aqueduct on 26 November 1805.

The Shropshire Volunteers appeared with a military band and cannon for firing salutes. Dignitaries made speeches, the band played 'loyal airs' and banners fluttered over the crowd. Some had poetic messages:

> Here conquer'd Nature owns Britannia's sway
> While Oceans' realms her matchless deeds display.

Others were rather more to the point: 'Success to the iron trade of Great Britain, of which Pontcysyllte aqueduct is a specimen.' Following the speeches, there was a procession of barges across the aqueduct, after which they turned round and came back again:

> The discharge from the guns, as the procession returned, the plaudits of the spectators (calculated at full 8,000), the martial music, the echo reverberating from the mountains, magnified the enchanting scene; and the countenance of every one present bespoke the satisfaction with which they completed this very useful and sumptuous work.[4]

The VIPs then retired for a 'sumptuous dinner', while the navvies were treated to roast sheep and 'an ample addition of beef and ale'.

A railway opening was no less exciting. This account of the ceremony on the Trent Valley Railway at Atherstone shows the navvies playing a starring role:

> The procession was formed about two o'clock headed by Mr. Wilday followed at a respectful distance by the 'navies' each supplied with a barrow and a spade and also with a new hat ... The different orders of Oddfellows, Druids and Freemasons followed next with their respective bands. A large number of the Charity School children brought up the rear. The scene of action was a

field belonging to Wilday in the middle of which he stood while the procession formed around him. The youngest children were in the first circle, the next tallest in the 2nd and so on then the different clubs. At a given signal all the navies wheeled their barrow-fulls into the circle and emptied them so as to form one large mound amid the cheers of the populace.[5]

After that the navvies went off to the local pubs, where seventeen sheep were being roasted, and 'all went to bed fully satisfied'.

At the end of the celebrations, the shareholders and proprietors could look forward to a profitable future when the revenues started coming in and the profits were shared out. Most of the leading engineers who were in charge of construction would have had more than one project on the go at any one time and now they simply had one less to worry about. For the navvies there was nothing to be done but to pack up their gear and march off in the hope of finding new work somewhere else in the country. The speeches had no doubt praised the engineers who had designed the route and thanked the promoters who had raised the money to pay for it, and no doubt they deserved the plaudits. But the navvies knew that it was their muscles and their strength that had dug the canal or built the line. The Industrial Revolution could never have taken place without the complex network of canals that covered the country, which provided Britain with the most efficient transport system it had had in centuries. In the nineteenth century the railways brought travel to millions who might never have strayed far from their town or village otherwise. And none of it would have been possible without tens of thousands of anonymous workers: the navvies.

END NOTES

Introduction

1. Frances Collier, *The Family Economy of the Working Classes in the Cotton Industry 1784–1833*, 1965.

Chapter One

1. Roy Palmer (ed.), *A Touch on the Times*, 1974.
2. *Ibid.*
3. Peter Lecount, *The History of the Railways connecting London and Birmingham*, 1839.
4. William Cobbett, *The Life and Adventures of Peter Porcupine*, 1796.
5. Quoted in Pamela Horn, *Labouring Life in the Victorian Countryside*, 1976.
6. *Annals of Agriculture*, 1786, quoted in Anthony Bird, *Roads and Vehicles*, 1969.
7. Arthur Young, *General View of the County of Oxfordshire*, 1813.
8. A.W. Skempton, 'Engineering on the English River Navigations to 1760' in Mark Baldwin and Anthony Burton (eds), *Canals a New Look*, 1984.

Chapter Two

1. W. Tatham, *The Political Economy of Inland Navigation*, 1799.
2. Anon., *A History of Inland Navigation*, 1779.
3. Samuel Smiles, *Lives of the Engineers*, Vol.1, 1862.
4. Coventry Canal Minute Book, 9 March 1768.
5. *Aris's Birmingham Gazette*, 1 June 1767.
6. Revd S. Shaw, *A Tour of the West of England in 1788*, 1789.

7. Quoted in Harry Hanson, *Canal People*, 1978.
8. Second Report of the Committee for Making and Maintaining the Caledonian Canal, 17 May 1805.
9. Engineers' Reports to the Management Committee, Kennet & Avon Canal Company, 1804.
10. *Morning Chronicle*, 11 April 1793.

Chapter Three

1. Quoted in Charles Hadfield, *The Canal Age*, 1968.
2. Robert Southey, *Journal of a Tour in Scotland in 1817*, 1829.
3. *Gentleman's Magazine*, September 1788.
4. Mr Millar's Reports to the Lancaster Canal Committee, 24 January 1794.
5. *Ibid.*, 6 May 1794.
6. Letter quoted in Anon., *A History of Inland Navigation*, 1779.
7. Quoted in Humphrey Household, *The Thames and Severn Canal*, 1969. This book contains a full account of the whole construction period.
8. Prof. R.B. Schofield, 'The Construction of the Huddersfield Narrow Canal 1794–1811', *Transactions of the Newcomen Society*, Vol.53, 1981–82.
9. Coventry Canal Minute Book, 29 August 1769.
10. *Ibid.*, 14 November 1769.
11. Lancaster Canal Letter Book, 2 February 1793.
12. Mr Millar's Reports, 2 September 1794.
13. Quoted in Hadfield, *op. cit.*
14. *Annual Register*, April 1811.
15. *Canal Boatman's Magazine*, Vol.1, No.1, 1829.
16. Mr Eastburn's Report to the Lancaster Canal Committee, 30 May 1796.
17. Leeds and Liverpool Canal Committee Minute Book, 3 January 1771.
18. Quoted in Charles Hadfield, *British Canals*, 7th edn, 1984.
19. Evidence given to Parliament by William Hallam, 25 February 1778.
20. 'General Ludd's Triumph' in Roy Palmer (ed.), *A Touch on the Times*, 1974.
21. *Carlisle Journal*, 18 July 1820, quoted in David Renishaw, *The Carlisle Navigation Canal*, 1997.
22. Second Report of the Caledonian Canal Committee, 17 May 1805.

Chapter Four

1. Samuel Homfray to Simon Goodrich, 27 February 1804.
2. Quoted in L.T.C. Rolt, *George and Robert Stephenson*, 1960.
3. Quoted in Anthony Burton, *The Rainhill Story*, 1980.
4. Rolt, *op. cit.*

5. *Liverpool Mercury*, 10 August 1827.
6. Fanny Kemble, *Records of a Girlhood*, 1878.

Chapter Five

1. C. Henry Warren, *Happy Countryman*, 1939.
2. *Illustrated London News*, 30 December 1854.
3. Arthur Helps, *Life & Labours of Mr. Brassey*, 1872.
4. John Francis, *A History of the English Railway*, 1851.
5. Samuel Smiles, *Story of the Life of George Stephenson*, 1857.
6. London & Birmingham Railway: Contractors' Wages and Petty Cash Book 1833–4.
7. *Felix Farley's Bristol Journal*, 9 March 1839.
8. *Ibid.*, 13 July 1839.
9. Helps, *op. cit.*

Chapter Six

1. Arthur Helps, *Life & Labours of Mr. Brassey*, 1872.
2. John Francis, *A History of the English Railway*, 1851.
3. Evidence to the Committee to Inquire into the Conditions of the Labourers Employed in the Construction of Railways, 1846 (hereafter referred to as 1846 Committee).
4. *Ibid.*
5. James Richardson, contractor on the Bishop Auckland & Weardale Railway (BA & WR), undated.
6. Francis, *op. cit.*
7. Ralph Lawson, BA & WR, undated.
8. I.K. Brunel letter book, 10 April 1839.
9. Full account in David Brooke, 'The "Great Commotion" at Mickleton, July 1851', *Journal of the Railway and Canal Historical Society*, Vol. XXX, part 2, 1990.
10. Darlington and Barnard Castle Railway papers.
11. Terry Coleman, *The Railway Navvies*, 1965.
12. *Felix Farley's Bristol Journal*, 28 April 1838.

Chapter Seven

1. Georgina Battiscombe, *Shaftesbury*, 1975.
2. Statistics from Kenneth Hudson, *Building Materials*, 1972.
3. Frederick S. Williams, *Our Iron Rails*, 1852.

4. Robert Rawlinson, evidence to the 1846 Committee.

5. Henry Lacey Pomfret, evidence to the 1846 Committee.

6. Rawlinson, *op. cit.*

7. *Felix Farley's Bristol Journal*, 8 August 1840.

8. Report on the Bishop Auckland & Weardale Railway, 1841.

9. Thomas Jackson, evidence to the 1846 Committee.

10. Charles Dickens, *Dombey and Son*, 1846.

11. Williams, *op. cit.*

12. The full story is told in L.T.C. Rolt, *George and Robert Stephenson*, 1967.

13. Anthony Murray, *The Forth Railway Bridge*, 1983.

Chapter Eight

1. *Felix Farley's Bristol Journal*, 27 July 1839.

2. *Ibid.*, 18 May 1839.

3. *Ibid.*, 18 July 1840.

4. *Ibid.*, 9 February 1839.

5. George Meason, *The Illustrated Guide to the Great Western Railway*, 1852.

6. Leeds & Thirsk Railway Report Book, December 1846.

7. Olinthus J. Vignoles, *Life of Charles Blacker Vignoles*.

8. Report on the Sheffield & Manchester Railway Company, 20 February 1837.

9. Quoted in Terry Coleman, *The Railway Navvies*, 1965.

10. Thomas A. Walker, *The Severn Tunnel*, 1888.

Chapter Nine

1. Quoted in David Philips, *Crime and Authority in Victorian England*, 1977.

2. F.R. Conder, *Personal Recollections of English Engineers*.

3. John Francis, *A History of the English Railway*, 1851.

4. F.B. Head, *Stokers and Pokers*, 1849.

5. *Preston Pilot*, 26 May 1838.

6. Police Inspector's Report, 23 November 1847.

7. Papers read before the Statistical Society of Manchester, quoting John Robertson, 18 November 1845.

8. Quoted in David Brooke, *The Railway Navvy*, 1983.

Chapter Ten

1. Quoted in J.L. and Barbara Hammond, *The Town Labourer*, 1917.

2. Evidence to the 1846 Committee.
3. Trent Valley Railway Letters, 1845–6.
4. *Felix Farley's Bristol Journal*, 7 February 1846.
5. *Ibid.*, 16 May 1846.
6. John Francis, *A History of the English Railway*, 1851.
7. The Vicar of Batley to the Leeds & Dewsbury Railway Company, 1 May 1846.

Chapter Eleven

1. Quoted in Cecil Woodham-Smith, *The Reason Why*, 1953.
2. Sir Henry Clifford, *Letters from the Crimea*, 1953.
3. Quoted in R.K. Middlemas, *The Master Builders*, 1963.
4. Clifford, *op. cit.*
5. *Illustrated London News*, March 1855.
6. Brunel to Brunton, 2 April 1855.

Chapter Twelve

1. Bagge to Telford, 2 April 1810.
2. James Simpson to John Simpson, 7 November 1814.
3. Robert Young, *Timothy Hackworth and the Locomotive*, 1923.
4. Quoted in N.W. Webster, *Joseph Locke: Railway Revolutionary*, 1978.
5. Mackenzie Papers, 25 April 1842.
6. Figures from David Brooke, *William Mackenzie*, 2004.
7. Arthur Helps, *Life & Labours of Mr. Brassey*, 1872.
8. *Ibid.*
9. *Ibid.*
10. W. Lloyd, *A Railway Pioneer*, 1900.
11. C.O. Burge, *The Adventures of a Civil Engineer*, 1909.
12. John Brunton's Book, 1939.
13. 'Great Indian Peninsula Railway', *Proceedings of the Institution of Civil Engineers*.
14. J.H. Patterson, *Man Eaters of Tsavo*, 1907.
15. The full story is told in Dee Brown, *Hear the Lonesome Whistle Blow*, 1977, from which all the quotes are taken.
16. Helps, *op. cit.*
17. *Ibid.*

Chapter Thirteen

1. Carol Hardie, 'The building of the "Big Ditch", the story of the Manchester Ship Canal', *The Victorian Society Liverpool Group News Letter*, December 2010.
2. Many of Newton's photographs are reproduced in L.T.C. Rolt, *The Making of a Railway: Building the Great Central*, 1971 (republished 1993).
3. The full story is told in Anthony Burton and John Scott-Morgan, *Britain's Light Railways*, 1985.
4. *Annual Register*, 1805.
5. Trent Valley Railway letters, 22 November 1846.

INDEX